Building More Dances

Blueprints for Putting Movements Together

Susan McGreevy-Nichols
Roger Williams Middle School
Providence, Rhode Island

Helene Scheff
Chance to Dance
East Greenwich, Rhode Island

Marty Sprague
Roger Williams Middle School
Providence, Rhode Island

Human Kinetics

Library of Congress Cataloging-in-Publication Data

McGreevy-Nichols, Susan, 1952-
    Building more dances : blueprints for putting movements together / Susan
McGreevy-Nichols, Helene Scheff, Marty Sprague.
        p. cm.
    Includes bibliographical references and index.
    ISBN 0-88011-973-X
    1. Dance for children--Study and teaching (Elementary) 2. Dance--Study and teaching
(Secondary) 3. Choreography--Study and teaching (Elementary) 4. Choreography--Study
and teaching (Secondary) 5. Movement education. I. Scheff, Helene, 1939- II. Sprague,
Marty, 1950- III. Title.

GV1799 .M313 2001
792.8'071--dc21   2001024835

ISBN: 0-88011-973-X

National Dance Content Standards 1-7 (pp. 6-9)—This quote is reprinted from *The National Standards for Dance Education: What Every Young American Should Know and Be Able to Do in the Arts* with permission of the National Dance Association (NDA) an association of the American Alliance for Health, Physical Education, Recreation and Dance. The original source may be purchased from: National Dance Association, 1900 Association Drive, Reston, VA 20191-1599; or phone (703) 476-3421.

National Standards for Physical Education 1-7 (pp. 9-13)—Reprinted from *Moving Into The Future: National Standards for Physical Education*, (1995) with permission from the National Association for Sport and Physical Education (NASPE), 1900 Association Drive, Reston, VA 20191-1599.

Acquisitions Editor: Judy Patterson Wright, PhD; **Managing Editor:** Amy Stahl; **Assistant Editor:** Derek Campbell; **Copyeditor:** Bonnie Pettifor; **Proofreader:** Jim Burns; **Permission Manager:** Dalene Reeder; **Graphic Designer:** Nancy Rasmus; **Graphic Artist:** Kathleen Boudreau-Fuoss; **Cover Designer:** Jack W. Davis; **Art Manager:** Craig Newsom; **Illustrator:** Dick Flood; **Printer:** Versa Press

Printed in the United States of America   10 9 8 7 6 5 4 3 2 1

Human Kinetics
Web site: www.humankinetics.com

United States: Human Kinetics, P.O. Box 5076, Champaign, IL 61825-5076
800-747-4457
e-mail: humank@hkusa.com

Canada: Human Kinetics, 475 Devonshire Road Unit 100, Windsor, ON N8Y 2L5
800-465-7301 (in Canada only)
e-mail: orders@hkcanada.com

Europe: Human Kinetics, Units C2/C3 Wira Business Park, West Park Ring Road, Leeds LS16 6EB, United Kingdom
+44 (0) 113 278 1708
e-mail: hk@hkeurope.com

Australia: Human Kinetics, 57A Price Avenue, Lower Mitcham, South Australia 5062
08 8277 1555
e-mail: liahka@senet.com.au

New Zealand: Human Kinetics, P.O. Box 105-231, Auckland Central
09-523-3462
e-mail: hkp@ihug.co.nz

Contents

Preface

In our first book, the well-received *Building Dances: A Guide to Putting Movements Together,* we developed a basic method of teaching dance through the "making" of dances. This book, *Building More Dances,* expands on our first book, providing more tools to help you teach students to build dances: more dance construction models, more ideas for creativity, and more ideas for lesson plans. In short, *Building More Dances* takes you further in the teaching of dance and dance-making.

Note that you need not have read or used *Building Dances* to make good use of *Building More Dances.* Each book stands alone, yet each complements the other. Both books offer a wealth of teaching material to guide you—whether you're a novice or seasoned dance educator—as you bring the thrill of creating and performing to your students.

Specifically, *Building More Dances* includes features from *Building Dances,* such as More Deal-a-Dance cards, new dance construction models, the seven steps of building a dance, and expanded assessment ideas. We have also included discussions of dance-making structures (forms), how to integrate movement skills and elements, and how to use music and simple props, scenery, and costumes to enhance student performances. In keeping with the current drive to develop standards-based curricula, this book includes an introduction to the standards and how dance curricula may help your students meet these standards.

Beyond these basic expansions, *Building More Dances* brings you more plans and materials for lessons. Geared to be adaptable to every level (K-12), sample activities model how you may use each lesson at the various levels of development. This book is both user-friendly to those who are using our approach for the first time as well as challenging to those who have worked with our approach before.

Purpose

The primary focuses of this book are to get children to make dances (to choreograph) and to raise the comfort level of all educators, no matter their past experiences with dance education. By simply working on these activities, you will become more comfortable with dabbling in dance-making. A secondary focus is to acquaint you with the National Dance Standards (from the National Standards for Arts Education, Music Educators National Conference [MENC] 1994) and the

National Standards for Physical Education (National Association for Sport and Physical Education [NASPE] 1995) and show you how to build your curriculum to support these standards. Thirdly, as mentioned earlier, the book is a resource of more dance construction models and the tools needed to build them. Tying all these areas of focus together, each model's lesson refers to the standard(s) it addresses.

Jump In!

Lastly, we want to dispel any fears you may have about the complexity of dance-building, or *choreography*. In this book are all the proper tools and foundations to make the process user-friendly. It is our experience that our approach significantly increases the level of comfort teachers feel regarding dance-making. Even more importantly, we have designed this book to help you get your students actively involved in the dance-building process—engaging not only their bodies but also their minds. Indeed, dance and dance education should engage the whole child.

To ensure that the material in this book is easy to use, relevant, and effective, we have had the dance construction models pilot-tested with preschool through high school students. These models have been used with children in a theater camp, a non-English–speaking children's program, in recreation programs, and in classrooms like yours. They have been used at the college level in teacher preparation programs of dance, physical education, theater, and music. Some models have been used with senior citizens. They have been used as classroom exercises and developed to performance level. While nothing here is "prefab," this book puts the systems in place for you and your students to make wonderful dances.

Your field of expertise, the level of your approach, and the age or ability level of your students does not matter. This book includes hours, days, and weeks of materials. Our combined experience, the benefits of pilot-testing, your strengths, and student research and creativity come together—and come alive. Dance and build, dance and teach, dance and create, but above all—dance and enjoy!

Acknowledgments

We wish to acknowledge and thank the following people: Stephen Provenzo, principal of Roger Williams Middle School in Providence, Rhode Island; Gerri Lallo, full-time dance instructor at Roger Williams Middle School; students at Roger Williams Middle School; South County Players' Children's Theatre; fifth-grade students of Smoketown Elementary School in Lancaster, Pennsylvania; and participants at local, regional, national, and international conferences, where we presented our raw material to patient and receptive audiences. From their responses came *Building More Dances*.

How to Use This Book: Construction Tips for Building Dances

This book follows in the footsteps of *Building Dances,* incorporating a hands-on approach to the mechanics and art of building more dances. First, each part of the book (I through VII) gives you an overview of an aspect of dance-making and offers a summary for easy reference. Then, in part VIII, dance construction models contain both the blueprints for and examples of age-appropriate dance-making activities.

Special Features

One special feature of this book is that we outline and compare the National Dance Standards and the National Standards for Physical Education. In addition, each dance construction model clearly lists which standard(s) it addresses. To round out our approach to assessment, we explain and suggest model assessments specific to each dance construction model, such as portfolio evidence, criteria, and rubrics.

Another special feature is a new set of 108 cards to support all the dance construction models as well as serve as the focal point of More Deal-a-Dance (see page 91). You may also use this set of cards in conjunction with the original Deal-a-Dance cards found in *Building Dances.*

Building the Dances

In *Building More Dances,* eight parts guide you through the process of creating dances with your classes:

- Part I, "Starting With Building Codes: Using Standards and Curricula," introduces you to the standards and commonly used terms. An "action plan" helps you align curriculum with standards.
- Part II, "Pouring the Foundation: Standards As Underpinning for Curricula," defines and compares the national standards for dance and physical education.
- Part III, "Stocking Up on Building Supplies: Nuts and Bolts of Movement," defines and gives examples of the movement skills and movement elements used in this book.

- Part IV, "Construction Time! Seven Steps to Building a Dance," provides a system for building a dance that includes the following seven steps:

  1. Choosing the subject matter
  2. Exploring and selecting movements
  3. Coordinating music and movement
  4. Exploring possibilities
  5. Refining and memorizing dance-making
  6. Adding the finishing touches
  7. Performing the dance

- Part V, "Framing and Plastering: Outlining and Filling In Your Dance Ideas," gives you examples of dance structures (forms), processes, and elements, expanding and completing the dances to meet standards and be "architecturally" interesting.

- Part VI, "Adding Architectural Details: Effects That Affect Meaning," helps you understand how music, costumes, props, lighting, and scenery add dimensions to any dance, making a good dance really special.

- Part VII, "Being the Building Inspector: Making Sure Dance Work Is Sound," is about the different ways of assessing student work, offering you valuable information and tools.

- Part VIII, "Building More Dances From Sample Blueprints: Dance Construction Models," includes 23 all-new dance construction models, encompassing individual lessons and multiple lessons, all of which you may develop into age-appropriate units. Described in the following list, each activity supports both the National Dance Standards and the National Standards for Physical Education (see appendix on page 115):

  - **Blueprint Dance**—This model takes students from creating forms and shapes on paper with pens, pencils, and crayons to re-creating their drawings through movement phrases. Integrated with math and art, drawings come to life.

  - **Carnivale**—This model takes the premise of a festival, such as Carnivale or Mardi Gras, to create a school-wide celebration.

  - **Communication Dance**—How have we communicated from the beginning of time to our present high-tech approaches? Research and creativity combine to inspire movement and dances.

  - **Concepts and Basic Skills Dance**—This model teaches and models age-appropriate skills that students should know.

  - **Countries Dance**—This model shows students how to create a dance or dances based on their research of a particular country or region.

  - **Create-a-Line Dance**—This model takes line dancing to a new level by requiring students to invent movements, create movement patterns, and then incorporate these to fit a piece of music.

  - **Dance-a-Quote**—Quotes from famous people and famous quotes are now remembered nonverbally through this model.

- **Dance-a-Warm-Up**—Why is warming up important and how interesting can this activity become with student creativity? This model gives you and your students the answers.

- **Dance Is in the Bag**—This model helps students build verbal storytelling skills while creating dances. It also helps build self-confidence and independent thought while honing interpersonal communication skills. Dances may become as simple or as complicated as you want them to be.

- **Dance Through History**—This model takes a particular person, date, or place in history and creates a dance to represent the subject.

- **Dance Through Time**—Students explore different periods in history and create dances, based on the facts they have learned. This model also helps students develop a better sense of why and how people in different time periods might have danced.

- **Dancing at the Joint**—In this model, students explore the various types of movement made at joints and how they may link these movements to form a dance.

- **Field Trip Dance**—Whether you actually go on a field trip or take a "virtual" field trip, you and your students can build a dance about the experience.

- **Have a Healthy Heart Dance**—This model takes aerobic exercise and routines and makes the dance-making process a fun game, linking the three parts of an effective and safe aerobic workout into one healthy heart activity.

- **Map-a-Dance**—This model uses maps to inspire dances while encouraging teamwork, enhancing problem-solving skills, and stimulating creativity. Specifically, maps and trails determine pathways for movement patterns and direct the theme.

- **Mask Dance**—This model uses masks to inspire dance-making while teaching students how and why masks are used in different cultures. This model makes it easy for you and your colleagues to combine the worlds of visual arts, history, and dance.

- **More Deal-a-Dance**—This model provides a new set of "playing" cards in four categories (see pages 91 through 92): More Creative Movement Suggestions, More Sport and Game Movements, More Elements That Change Movement, and More Dance Techniques and Basic Movements. You and your students may use the information on both the fronts and backs of these cards as sources for all the movements needed to build any of the dance construction models and as the sources for building student dance vocabularies.

- **Mythology Dance**—This model encourages students to learn about myths and research details of myths to create dances about the myths and characters. You may also demonstrate how to analyze characters' behavior and portray physical traits.

- **Rhythmatron Dance**—In this model, students develop the ability to respond to changes in rhythms, tempos, and syncopations.

- **Scavenger Hunt Dance**—This model uses collected items to inspire dances. The process of collecting encourages teamwork, enhances problem-solving and research skills, and hones observation skills.

- **Sculpture and Shape Dance**—Two- and three-dimensional inanimate objects come to life through movement through this model.

- **Seesaw Dance**—This model demonstrates the pulling action of muscles and how muscles move bones.

- **Social Studies Dance**—Students research major topics and concepts, including prejudice, cause and effect, government, civics, transportation, community, and industry; then students mold these into movement and dance.

PART I

Starting With Building Codes:
Using Standards and Curricula

General Introduction to Standards

Whoever you are, whatever part of the country, whatever district you are in, whatever your student population, you are now being asked to define your educational goals and content choices in relation to standards and/or outcomes.

This is no different from a builder who is required to comply with building codes when creating a blueprint. And just as building codes determine your design, dimensions, and materials, standards should determine curricula.

The main purpose of this book is to get children to make dances (to *choreograph*). The dance-making process is a major aspect embodied in both the National Dance Standards and the National Standards for Physical Education. Approaching these standards through dance-making can unify your dance activities while also providing many hours of fun, fitness, and learning.

Much has been written about national standards related to physical activity in recent years; here we summarize the developments most relevant to this book. Two major documents helped shape the standards as we know and use them today. *National Standards for Arts Education: What Every Young American Should Know and Be Able to Do in the Arts* (1994) was developed by the Consortium of National Arts Education Associations (CNAEA). In 1995, a similar document, *Moving Into the Future: National Standards for Physical Education: A Guide to Content and Assessment,* was published by the National Association for Sport and Physical Education (NASPE). Both set forth some similar principles and expectations, and physical educators have widely accepted the guidelines they offer. Indeed, these standards have become a crucial element in providing children with a well-rounded education in which high achievement is the focus.

Standards should help mold the content of each classroom activity you select. Student work is the outcome of a particular activity. It should be assessment and documentation of student work, not the classroom activities themselves, that demonstrate a student has achieved a standard. Thus, the standards provide a basis on which you may assess student work and achievements. Ultimately, assessment should feed back into content selection as you strive to choose activities that will further help students reach the standards.

Developed in consensus with several standards documents, the following list of terms and explanations offers a brief overview of the terminology commonly used in reference to standards. (*Note:* Even within a given discipline, we find variations of definitions; however, the more that focus groups struggle with the meanings of the standards, the clearer the definitions are becoming.)

- Standards—This is a general term describing what a student should know and be able to do. In other words, standards are a body of knowledge, skills, and understanding a student should have attained in a particular area. A student should have met each standard by the time the student completes his or her secondary education. A well-written standard gives parents, students, teachers, and administrators a clear picture of expectations.

- Content standards—These standards specify what a student should know and be able to do in a specific discipline such as physical education, science, math, etc. Collectively, the content standards of a subject area address the skills, knowledge, and processes essential to mastering that discipline.

- Benchmark—This term describes specific skills and knowledge a student should achieve by the end of a specific grade level. In other words, they are outlining the specific developmental components of a subject area. Think of each benchmark as a step in the sequence toward achieving the standard. Benchmarks may be written as statements of information and skills, as performance activities, or as performance tasks.

Aligning Curriculum With Standards

Building codes guide builders as they develop their blueprints. In turn, the blueprints give the basic outline of how the building will look and function. Likewise, standards can *support* the curriculum (see figure 1.1). Your curriculum is simply what you and your students do during the school year in your classroom.

At this point, we need to clear up some frequently observed confusion between the two words *curriculum* and *framework*. Is framework just a "new and improved" way of saying curriculum? Here's our take on these two terms:

- Curriculum—This is defined as a "regular or a particular course of study." It is sequential steps through a course of study to learn a specific body of knowledge. While standards provide educational goals, a curriculum defines how those goals will be achieved.

Figure 1.1   A strong foundation leads to more successful student work.

- Framework—This is a guide to use in planning, supporting, implementing, and evaluating programs. While a framework does not detail curriculum (e.g., does not answer the question, "What do I do with my students on Monday?"), it identifies the important standards-based concepts, principles, and content for a specific subject. Along with standards, frameworks change over time as technology, education, and society at large evolve. Schools and teachers may choose and use a wide array of curriculum materials, instructional strategies, and assessment and system support within a framework. In turn, a framework may help staff examine, revise, and support existing curriculum. It is important to note that frameworks may include the standards that are specified by the school district.

Armed with this information, you can determine how standards and curriculum affect the everyday teaching and learning in your classroom. Here is an action plan for aligning your curriculum with standards, helping you find and fill in the missing pieces:

1. List the standards you are being asked to meet.
2. Look at your yearlong curriculum.
3. List what pieces of student work are already required by your present curriculum.
4. Determine which student work aligns with which standards.
5. Figure out what student work is already included and what student work is missing.
6. Revise curriculum and student work requirements to fill in the missing pieces.
7. Revise and sequence your everyday teaching and learning to facilitate the student work, which, in turn, will satisfy the standards.

After following this action plan, you will find that your curriculum already includes many of the components—skills, knowledge, concepts, and processes—that will help students achieve the standards. It then becomes a relatively simple matter to add the missing curriculum content to help students meet each standard.

Summary

Standards—and striving for them—are key components in most educational reform efforts. Moreover, realigning curriculum, teaching, learning, and assessment with accepted standards is an essential undertaking in these efforts. Documented, assessed student work *resulting* from classroom activities—not the classroom activities themselves—demonstrates the achievement of each standard. In other words, you can plan and teach all the right things, but you must ensure students are learning the content—and that you have documented this learning.

PART II

Pouring the Foundation:
Standards As Underpinning for Curricula

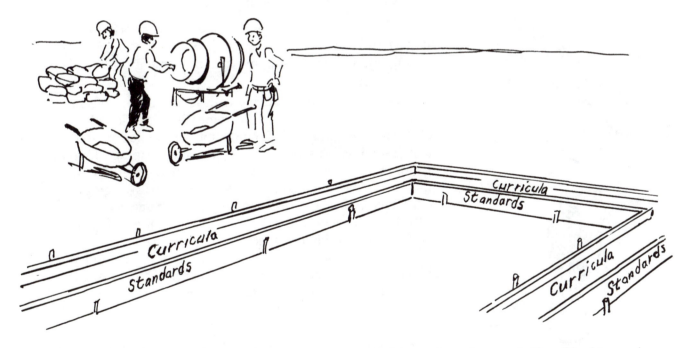

Defining the National Dance Content Standards and the National Standards for Physical Education

To be able to use the National Dance Content Standards and the National Standards for Physical Education effectively in teaching and learning, you must first understand them. When relevant we quote directly from the standards' documents, then explain further what the standard means to real teaching-learning settings, real students, and real student work.

Figure 2.1   Basic movement skill . . . JUMP!

Figure 2.2   Proper alignment is the key to balance.

The National Dance Content Standards

• National Dance Content Standard 1 (Consortium of National Arts Education Associations [CNAEA] 1994, p. 55): Identifying and demonstrating movement elements and skills in performing dance.

This content standard deals with learning of the technical vocabulary as it pertains to movement skills, principles, and elements. *Movement skills* include both locomotor movements (e.g., hopping, walking, running, jumping, leaping, skipping, galloping, sliding; see figure 2.1) and nonlocomotor movements (e.g., bending, twisting, stretching, and swinging).

Movement principles include alignment, balance (see figure 2.2), initiation of movement, isolations, weight transfer, takeoff and landing, and fall and recovery.

Movement elements include shape, the positions and ways a body is used; space, how and where the movement takes place; time, the time it takes to do a movement or a movement pattern; and force (energy), the "quality" of the movement (see figure 2.3).

• National Dance Content Standard 2 (CNAEA 1994, p. 56): Understanding choreographic principles, processes, and structures.

This content standard expects students to integrate dance knowledge and skills into the dance-making process. Specifically, students should work cooperatively while creating dances based on their own ideas as they manipulate the movement by

Figure 2.3   Groups make interesting shapes.

changing the time, space, force, and energy. Students should also learn dance-making principles, such as contrast, complementary, variety, and transitional movements (see figure 2.4); dance-making processes, such as reordering and chance; dance-making structures or forms, such as AB, ABA, rondo, theme and variation, motif and development, canon, narrative, and suite.

• National Dance Content Standard 3 (CNAEA 1994, p. 56): Understanding dance as a way to create and communicate meaning.

Figure 2.4   Dancers use complementary shapes to create images.

Figure 2.5 Communicating meaning— "Oh, woe is me!"

This content standard deals with thinking, creating, and communicating through dance. Specifically, students should have to think to develop an idea. They must be creative to interpret the idea through the kinesthetic avenue. Communication results from the interaction between dance-maker and dancer(s) and their audience (see figure 2.5). It is the responsibility of the dance-maker to get the dancer(s) to make the original idea clear enough for the audience to unravel.

• National Dance Content Standard 4 (CNAEA 1994, p. 56): Applying and demonstrating critical and creative thinking skills in dance.

This content standard deals with problem inventing and solving. Students should use creative-thinking skills in dance by generating, inventing, conceiving, experimenting with, and exploring movement (see figure 2.6). In addition, students should use critical-thinking skills to manipulate movement by organizing, judging, refining, analyzing, and shaping movement. In short, to meet Content Standard 4, students must not only create a problem but also be able to find several solutions to the problem and, ultimately, choose the best solution.

• National Dance Content Standard 5 (CNAEA 1994, p. 57): Demonstrating and understanding dance in various cultures and historical periods.

This content standard encourages students to learn about and perform dances from different cultures and historical periods (see figure 2.7). They should come to understand how and why people dance(d) in different cultures and time periods.

Thus, you should know and teach that dance is one of the most basic actions that people do everywhere in the world. People dance for religious reasons and to celebrate, commune with their ancestors, commemorate, bring on or ward off spirits, cure diseases, and perform a rite of passage.

Figure 2.6 Problem: Create different shapes without breaking the chain.

Figure 2.7   Similar body shapes can be found among many different cultural dances.

• National Dance Content Standard 6 (CNAEA 1994, p. 58): Making connections between dance and healthful living.

This content standard encourages students to set personal goals for improving health-related fitness through dance, deciding on a course of action to meet these goals, and reflecting on their progress. Students should be able to explain how good nutrition, safety, and positive lifestyle choices can affect them as dancers (see figure 2.8).

• National Dance Content Standard 7 (CNAEA 1994, p. 58): Making connections between dance and other disciplines.

This content standard encourages students to create dances, inspired by many other disciplines. Indeed, students should be able to create and respond to dance by connecting to other disciplines and art forms, integrating skills and knowledge gained from other classes into their dance work. Fashion has always been an indicator of social mores. The "zoot suit" of the forties was a reaction to the end of World War II, and the dances showed the feeling of freedom (see figure 2.9).

Figure 2.8   Strengthening specific muscle groups.

Figure 2.9 Style is everything!

The National Standards for Physical Education

• National Standard for Physical Education 1: "Demonstrates competency in many movement forms and proficiency in a few movement forms" (NASPE 1995, p. 2). As stated in the NASPE (1995, p. 2) document, "The intent of this standard is the development of movement competence and proficiency." This standard fosters progressive development of movement skills and patterns: (1) motor skills, (2) motor patterns, (3) manipulative skills, or "hand-eye coordination," (4) combinations of the first three, and (5) specialized movement skills as needed for specific activities (e.g., specific dance step, catching with a glove; see figure 2.10).

• National Standard for Physical Education 2: "Applies movement concepts and principles to the learning and development of motor skills" (NASPE 1995,

Figure 2.10 Split leap and catching a fly.

The National Standards for Physical Education are reprinted from National Association for Sport and Physical Education 1995.

p. 2). "This standard concerns the ability of the learner to use cognitive information to understand and enhance motor skill acquisition and performance" (NASPE 1995, p. 2). This standard encourages students to apply and integrate previously learned skills and knowledge to new tasks, which, in effect, means they must learn and apply the patterns of "how to learn." As a result, students should also be able to evaluate and refine their own performances. For example, by learning to run correctly, you can adapt it to skills such as hurdle, broad jump, and gymnastic approaches.

• National Standard for Physical Education 3: "Exhibits a physically active lifestyle" (NASPE 1995, p. 2). "This standard should connect what is done in the physical education class with the lives of students outside of physical education" (NASPE 1995, p. 2). Students should be aware of the physical, social, and psychological benefits of physical education. To meet this standard, students should have positive attitudes toward physical activity and knowledge of how to develop a personal physical activity goal. In essence, this standard encourages students to understand, develop, and live active, healthy lifestyles (see figure 2.11).

• National Standard for Physical Education 4: "Achieves and maintains a health-enhancing level of physical fitness" (NASPE 1995, p. 3). "The intent of this standard is for the student to achieve a health-enhancing level of physical fitness" (NASPE 1995, p. 3). To achieve this standard, students must regularly participate in health-related fitness activities and be able to assess and analyze their progress toward individual fitness goals.

• National Standard for Physical Education 5: "Demonstrates responsible personal and social behavior in physical activity settings" (NASPE 1995, p. 3). "The intent of this standard is achievement of self-initiated behaviors that promote personal and group success in activity settings. These include safe practices, adherence to rules and procedures, etiquette, cooperation and teamwork, ethical behavior in sport, and positive social interaction" (NASPE 1995, p. 3).

The very nature of dance-making encourages cooperation and appropriate social behavior (see figure 2.12). Students should also understand and follow pertinent safety rules and cooperative-learning and dance etiquette.

Figure 2.11   Everyone can be physically active.

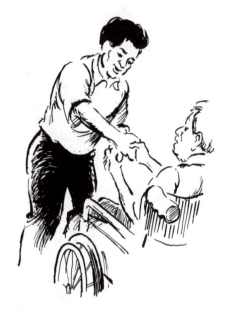

Figure 2.12 Circles enhance the feeling of community.

Figure 2.13 Respect and support differences.

• National Standard for Physical Education 6: "Demonstrates understanding and respect for differences among people in physical activity settings" (NASPE 1995, p. 3). "The intent of this standard is to develop respect for individual similarities and differences through positive interaction among participants in physical activity. Similarities and differences include characterizations of culture, ethnicity, motor performance, disabilities, physical characteristics (e.g., strength, size, shape), gender, race, and socio-economic status" (NASPE 1995, pp. 3-4).

Students should recognize how classmates are alike and different and accept everyone, participating in cooperative-learning physical activities willingly (see figure 2.13). In addition, as discussed on page 8 in regard to the National Dance Content Standard 5, students gain much from exploring the cultures of others.

• National Standard for Physical Education 7: "Understands that physical activity provides opportunities for enjoyment, challenge, self-expression, and social interaction" (NASPE 1995, p. 4) (see figure 2.14). "Physical activity can provide opportunity for self-expression and social interaction and can be enjoy-

Figure 2.14 Social dancing equals social interaction.

able, challenging, and fun" (NASPE 1995, p. 4). Certainly, dance-making provides opportunities for students to meet all the aspects of this standard.

Comparing the National Dance Content Standards and the National Standards for Physical Education

The content of dance is the total focus of the National Dance Content Standards. Dance as a physical activity is also addressed within the National Standards for Physical Education. We compare both sets of standards and show you how the two correlate. Once you understand how they work together, you can use them to design student work that meets both sets. First, though, let's look at those correlations.

As you compare the two documents, keep in mind that dance is truly an art form, an arts discipline, an aesthetic experience. Dance is a means of communication—communicating with others and communicating with one's own body. But dance is also a very physical activity. It makes you sweat! It is both a means of physical expression and physical challenge. Whether at the ballet barre or the parallel bars, both dancers and athletes are in constant competition with themselves, always striving for the next level of achievement and proficiency.

National Dance Content Standard 1 correlates with the National Standards for Physical Education 1 and 2. All three standards deal with competency in developing skills and knowledge.

National Dance Content Standard 2 correlates with National Standard for Physical Education 2. Both are concerned with application of the skills and knowledge attained in each entity's first standard. In a limited way, National Standard for Physical Education 7 also mentions dance-making as a form of self-expression and communication. The main focus of the dance standard, however, is the art of dance-making, which is creating something new from individual movements.

National Dance Content Standard 3 correlates with National Standard for Physical Education 7. Both these standards are concerned with student ability to communicate through movement.

National Dance Content Standard 4 correlates with National Standard for Physical Education 2. Both standards are concerned with learning and applying patterns of how to learn. The critical-thinking skill mentioned on the dance side is the same as is needed to evaluate and refine personal performance, mentioned on the physical education side.

National Dance Content Standard 5 correlates with National Standard for Physical Education 6. Both are concerned with respecting and understanding differences among people.

National Dance Content Standard 6 correlates with National Standards for Physical Education 3, 4, and 5. All these standards are concerned with practicing healthy lifestyles.

National Dance Content Standard 7 correlates with National Standard for Physical Education 5. Both are concerned with teamwork.

Table 2.1 summarizes the correlations between the two sets of standards.

The appendix outlines how the "blueprints"—dance construction models—this book provides explore and ultimately produce student work pertaining to a particular standard(s). The finished dance (a piece of student work), or the product of the dance-building process, can be the focus of your curriculum.

Table 2.1	How National Dance Content Standards Align With the National Standards for Physical Education	
National Dance Content Standard 1	National Standards for Physical Education 1 & 2
National Dance Content Standard 2	National Standards for Physical Education 2 & 7
National Dance Content Standard 3	National Standard for Physical Education 7
National Dance Content Standard 4	National Standard for Physical Education 2
National Dance Content Standard 5	National Standard for Physical Education 6
National Dance Content Standard 6	National Standards for Physical Education 3, 4, & 5
National Dance Content Standard 7	National Standard for Physical Education 5

Dances built using the dance construction models provide the curriculum content you can use to help your students meet these standards. Even though all the dance construction models address content within more than one standard, we feature which models best address which standards.

Student work produced by the various dance-building activities contained in this book will meet standards in a number of disciplines. We have used performance and content standards taken from the following: National Standards for Arts Education, National Standards for History, National Health Education Standards, the National Science Education Standards, National Geography Standards, National Standards for U.S. History, and New Standards Performance Standards. All these standards are available through the specific national professional associations and are also included in Kendall and Marzano's *Content Knowledge: A Compendium of Standards and Benchmarks for K-12 Education, 2nd ed.* The New Standards (performance standards in Science, Math, English Language Arts, and Applied Learning) are available through the National Center on Education and the Economy (202-783-3668) or through their Web site: **http://www.ncee.org**. These standards were created by national professional associations that serve the specific disciplines. Most states, provinces, and districts have either adopted national standards or have written their own versions. Check with your district administration to find out which standards you should be using. You can easily substitute your local standards for the national standards as you adapt the Blueprints for your own needs.

Summary

When we explore and compare the National Dance Content Standards and the National Standards for Physical Education, we see the direction to take in building a curriculum that includes dance. Indeed, standards are a strong foundation for designing student dance work as well as sound underpinnings for all teaching and learning. When you align curriculum with accepted standards, you will also see that you may then use each piece of student work to satisfy more than one standard in more than one content area. Specifically, the dance construction models in this book provide the means of producing student work that can satisfy many different standards. The desired end result is the same: a well-thought-out, well-performed piece of student work—a dance.

PART III

Stocking Up on Building Supplies:
Nuts and Bolts of Movement

Movement skills, principles, and elements are the nuts and bolts—the most vital components—of making dances. In *Building Dances*, we explored the basics of movement skills (locomotor and nonlocomotor movements) and movement elements (shape, space, time, and force). Here in *Building More Dances*, we go beyond the basics, exploring the skills, principles, and elements from other viewpoints.

Keep in mind that dance, like any other physical activity, requires a proper warm-up. You can use the following dance construction models: Dance-a-Warm-Up, Have a Healthy Heart Dance, and Dancing at the Joint to create proper warm-up activities (pages 63, 81, and 75, respectively. You can also refer to *Building Dances* (part I) for detailed safety tips and descriptions of the three main parts of a dance lesson: warm-up, activity, and cool-down.

Movement Skills

As mentioned earlier in the book, movement skills include locomotor movements, such as hopping, walking, running, jumping, leaping, skipping, galloping, and sliding. Movement skills also include nonlocomotor movements, such as bending, twisting, stretching, and swinging.

Movement Principles

Movement principles are the mechanics of movement. We suggest you introduce and incorporate them into the warm-up sections of classes that include movement. Understanding and mastering these principles help students perform specific dance movements they may later incorporate into the dance-making process. The following is a list of specific movement principles and their definitions:

- Alignment—This is the relationship of the bones of the body to the base of support and to the lines of gravity.
- Balance—This is the body's ability to hold a position without toppling over. Sometimes the performer can counterbalance the body, distributing weight equally on either side of the "center" of the body. Two or more performers may counterbalance each other as well.
- Initiation of movement—The start, or origin, of a movement; it can be *distal* (from the head or limbs) or *central* (from the torso).
- Articulation of isolated body parts—This is the movement of one body part while all other parts are still, such as rolling the wrist, moving the ribs sideways, or jutting the head forward.
- Weight shift—This happens when you transfer from one body support to another. Dancers shift weight from one foot to another. Gymnasts may also shift from one hand to another.
- Takeoff and landing—*Takeoff* is when the performer lifts the body off the floor (or other surface) and gains height. *Landing* is the body's taking its place back on the surface from which it started.
- Fall and recovery—This is when the body goes to a lower level and then returns back or up to the starting position.

Movement Elements

There are two ways of looking at the term "movement elements." In *Building Dances,* we categorized movement elements as "shape, space, time, and force."

Labanalysis, created by Rudolf von Laban and his followers, is another way of looking at and describing movement that many people in the dance field use. If you use both ways of looking at movement elements, your students' dance-making can only improve.

Labanalysis, with its descriptive definitions and vocabulary, is useful in observing, describing, and improving movement. You may use it in both dance and physical education, to increase the range of a body's mobility, efficiency, and expressive ability. In Labanalysis, *effort* is the "attitude" shown in the energy a performer exerts when executing a movement. It is "how" a movement is performed, or the "quality" of the movement. By "attitude" we mean your inner feeling toward the movement while performing it. For example, you can walk slowly as if it is a lazy summer day or you can walk slowly as if you are fearful that you are in danger.

Effort involves four elements: weight, time, space, and flow. We may describe *weight* as "strong" or "light." For example, a punch uses strong weight and a dab uses light weight. We may describe *time* as "sudden" or "sustained." A flick is sudden and a pressing action is sustained. We may describe *space* as "direct" or "indirect." Gliding uses direct space and floating uses indirect space. Combinations of these first three effort elements are called basic effort actions. See the More Deal-a-Dance cards (page 116) for a set of cards that encourages students to explore these eight actions. Divided into two groups of four, the cards emphasize "strong" weight versus "light" weight, helping students better understand effort actions in general.

Finally, we may describe the effort element of *flow* as "bound" or "free." For example, wringing is bound and slashing is free. More Deal-a-Dance also includes cards to encourage students to explore flow.

Summary

To build dances, students need to know about movement skills, principles, and elements. These are the essence of every dance creation—its nuts and bolts. Many students will intuitively incorporate these skills, principles, and elements into their work. However, knowing what they are doing and what effect their choices achieve make dance-makers more comfortable and confident. Indeed, students who know and can perform the basics are empowered to become better dance-makers.

PART IV

Construction Time!
Seven Steps to Building a Dance

7. Perform the dance
6. Add finishing touches
5. Refine and memorize dance
4. Explore possibilities
3. Coordinate music and movement
2. Explore and select movements
1. Choose subject matter

As with any other process, dance-making progresses through a logical sequence. In this part, we review, enhance, and upgrade descriptions and examples of the seven basic steps to building dances to demystify the process. New readers will get a comprehensive overview of the construction process. Readers of *Building Dances* will also find the expansion of this part helpful and inspiring. So grab your tool belt and begin the building process (see figure 4.1).

Figure 4.1 Just seven steps to completed student work.

Step 1: Choose the Subject Matter—Looking for Inspiration

The subject matter of your dance is your inspiration, and you can make a dance about anything. It can be about a story, theme, or topic. It can be the music or lyrics from a favorite song. It can be based on a science or social studies lesson. Look at the titles of the dance construction models for hints of how varied your choices of subject matter can be. Collect and store ideas for dances in your toolbox (e.g., file box or folder), and you will soon find you are never at a loss for dance ideas.

Step 2: Explore and Select Movements—Inventing Movement

After choosing your subject matter, you may now begin to explore movements to express this subject matter. Your approach may take a variety of forms. For example, you can brainstorm verbs (action words) dealing with the subject matter and then create movements that portray these words. Similarly, you can brainstorm descriptive words or phrases that illustrate and communicate your ideas, telling you how to perform your movements. The cards in More Deal-a-Dance (this book) and Deal-a-Dance (in *Building Dances*) are good sources of basic movements and dance skills you may combine or change to generate movements for your dance.

Another way you may explore movement is through improvisation, which is simply "playing" with movement. Start with one simple movement, and as you play with it, it inspires more movement. Soon, the movement grows into something more—a movement "phrase." A movement phrase is like a sentence, a complete thought. Ultimately, several movement sentences may become a movement "paragraph," or section of a dance.

You may notice that while students are exploring, they may come up with very literal movements. A handshake, for example, is a literal movement. Making an abstract movement out of a literal movement will open more possibilities for movement exploration. *Abstract movement* expresses a quality or characteristic apart from the real subject matter that you chose in Step 1. It should still contain the essential qualities, or "seed," of the idea you are exploring. An easy way to explain the difference between literal and abstract movement to students is to use a popcorn analogy: "When you look at unpopped popcorn it looks like corn and is corn. Then you pop it, and it becomes big and fluffy. However, it is still corn."

The following lists some ways to help students take literal movement into abstract movement using the literal movement of a handshake.

- Change the rhythm. For example, make the rhythm of the handshake uneven, e.g., instead of only going up and down, shake up, up, up, down).
- Change and/or vary the speed. For example, shake hands very slowly then extremely fast.
- Change and/or vary the size of the movement. For example, make the handshake so small you can barely see it and/or so large you have to move from a high to a low level.
- Repeat the movement over and over. For example, repeat the movement until it loses its significance as a gesture and becomes simply a movement.
- Use the same movement with a different body part. For example, do the handshake movement with your elbow, foot, or head.
- Do the opposite action and combine it with the original movement. For example, instead of facing the person you are greeting, move away as if to "ignore" the other person.
- Make a new unrelated movement and mix it in with the original movement. For example, spin on your toes and connect it with the handshake.
- Interrupt or have the movement take a detour to augment the original movement. For example, begin to shake hands, then use a locomotor movement to travel away and finally return to finish the handshake.
- Let the movement grow and change. For example, repeat the handshake until it starts to change and "follow it" wherever it might lead.

Note: Students need time to play with the literal movement to change it into the abstract. Plan this time into your lessons.

Step 3: Coordinate Music and Movement—Outlining and Organizing

When music is an integral part of the dance-building process, the structure appears stronger because it has this "mortar" to hold it together. In *Building Dances*, we discussed different ways of outlining the structure of the music and organizing movements within that structure. Many times, students may have to add, subtract, or rearrange the movement phrases to align the dance with the music. Likewise, you or your students may organize the music by using the lyrics or counting the beats. There are three ways to organize music: (1) organize into musical phrases, (2) organize by using the lyrics, or (3) counting sets of beats. These processes are described more fully in part II of *Building Dances*. Here, however, we update how to outline music, based on an interesting teaching experience we had.

In *Building Dances*, we charted out the music by using slashes (/) to indicate measures of music. There were four or eight beats, or counts, for each slash. When you chart out (count out) music, the resulting page could look something like this: |/////|. Everyone understood—or so we thought. When teaching this process to a class of eight-year-olds with limited English language skills, however, we learned otherwise. After the class, one little girl came up and said, "That was fun, but I make my eights like this ("8") not like that ("/")." Since then, we have revised how we chart music. To make reading the chart easier, if a measure has four counts, we use the numeral "4" in parentheses "(4)" for each set of four counts, "(8)" for each set of eight counts, and so on.

The following is an example of music outlined, using the lyrics for "Jack and Jill."

Jack and Jill
Phrase Dance beat
1   Jack (1) and Jill (2) went up (3) the hill (4),
2   To fetch (1) a pail (2) of wa- (3) ter (4).
3   Jack (1) fell down (2) and broke (3) his crown (4),
4   And Jill (1) came tum- (2) bling af- (3) ter (4).

Next is an example of organizing music by counting the beats.

Any popular song
Intro	8 8 8 8	(32 counts)
Theme A	8 8 8 8 8	(40 counts)
Theme B	8 8 8 8	(32 counts)
Transition	8 4	(12 counts)
Theme C	8 8 8 8	(32 counts for the chorus)
Theme A	8 8 8 8 8	(40 counts)
Theme B	8 8 8 8	(32 counts)
Transition	8 4	(12 counts)
Theme C	8 8 8 8	(32 counts for the chorus)
Theme D	8 8 8 8 8 8 8 8 8 8 8 8	(96 counts)
Theme A	8 8 8 8 8	(40 counts, including a fade)

Remember, see *Building Dances*, part II for more information on how to do this step.

Step 4: Explore Possibilities—Experimenting With Movement Components

In *Building Dances*, part III, we showed you how to alter or enhance dance-making by changing elements that impact the dances. For example, you could change the rhythm. Instead of accenting the first beat of each measure, you could alternate accenting beats with each measure like this: (**1**, 2, 3, 4) (1, **2**, 3, 4) (1, 2, **3**, 4) (1, 2, 3, **4**). You could also change formations (the placement of the dancers on the stage).

But now, when taking dance-building to the next level, take a more in-depth look into dance-making structures, principles, and elements. You and your students may use these to manipulate the movement phrases into dances. They also give you ways to potentially organize your dance material and add interest to a dance. In part V, we define the meanings of several dance-making structures, or forms. In addition, we explain a multitude of other dance-making elements so you and your students may explore the unlimited possibilities these give your dances.

Step 5: Refine and Memorize the Dance-Making—Practice, Practice, Practice!

Your job in this step is to make sure that the dancers are performing the dance-making as it was created and set (finalized). Whether you, a guest artist, or the students have set the dance-making, the dancers must stay true to the original concept and the final revisions as they rehearse. In addition, rehearsal may help prevent stage fright. When students have practiced a movement over and over, "muscle memory" kicks in, overriding nervousness.

Make rehearsals as effective as possible by having dancers practice transitions (within and between dances). Teach the dancers to get in and out of movement sections cleanly. In addition, do not allow students to repeat the same incorrect patterns. Stop, review, and have the students try again (see figure 4.2). Beyond these tips, what makes a good performer? Practice! What makes a good performance? Practice! Practice! Practice!

Figure 4.2   Practice, practice, practice!

Step 6: Add the Finishing Touches–Details Make a Difference

As we discuss in more detail in part VI of this book, you may add many details that may make a difference to the finished performance. After the students find the inspiration, they may research costumes, props, and set pieces to enhance the finished dance or become an integral part of the piece (see figure 4.3). Encourage them to come up with appropriate designs, given the particular theme.

Figure 4.3   Different occupations are clearly implied by the addition of these costumes.

Step 7: Perform the Dance–Exhibition at Its Best!

The dance is completed. Students have rehearsed it to public-performance level. You and your students have seen to the finishing touches. You have decided to have them share it with an audience, either formally or informally. The process is complete, and now come the accolades. Students have much to gain from both all the hard work and the actual performance: the reward of hard work, the joy of succeeding, and the thrill of becoming someone or something other than yourself (if only for a little while)—to name only a few.

Summary

The dance construction models are good resources for ways to use the seven steps of the dance-making process, as outlined in this part. With these steps as your guide, you and your students can experience the success of creating and performing a truly well-crafted dance piece, employing skills, principles, and elements of movement and dance-making. Next, part V explores how to fill in more details to make your dances even more interesting.

PART V

Framing and Plastering:
Outlining and Filling
In Your Dance Ideas

In part IV, we showed you how to put all the main pieces of a dance together. Now in part V, we look at ways to further develop and organize movement into dances. Just as a building has a frame, a dance should have a dance-making structure, or form, to organize and support the main idea. Then you can think of the dance-making processes as the hallways that take you from room to room and the stairways that take you from floor to floor.

The dance-making elements fill in and embellish the main idea just as plastering fills in the framing of a house. These additional details keep the dancers, the movement, and the audience's attention focused on the main idea. And as plastering or stucco adds texture and ornamentation to walls, so elements add interest to a dance.

Dance-Making Structures, or Forms

Once you have developed material (dance movements and movement phrases), you need to organize it within some type of structure. Specifically, no matter what the form, all dances should have a beginning shape, pose, or entrance; a middle section, consisting of development or exploration of the main idea; and a clear ending, consisting of a shape or pose, or an exit. The following list names and explains the various types of structures commonly used in dance-making. Note that, in some instances, they are very similar to musical structures.

- Canon—A canon, or round, can be described as singing "Row, row, row your boat" in parts but using movement in place of the lyrics.
- AB—This is (A), a movement phrase, and (B), a new movement phrase.
- ABA—This is (A), a movement phrase; (B), a new movement phrase; and a return to (A), the first movement phrase.
- Rondo—This pattern is (A) (B) (A) (C) (A) (D) (A). (A) is the primary movement phrase and is constantly being repeated and interspersed between other phrases. (B), (C), and (D) should be different from each other and from (A).
- Theme and variation—This is a movement phrase or section of a dance with subsequent movement phrases or sections created as variations of the original. We may write this as follows: (A), (A1), (A2), (A3).
- Narrative—This form tells a story or conveys an idea. The sequence, or development, of the story determines the structure of the dance.
- Collage—This form consists of a series of movement phrases that are often unrelated but have been brought together to create a single dance with a beginning, a middle, and an end.
- Accumulation—The following model best describes this form (each number represents a distinct movement or movement phrase): (1); (1, 2); (1, 2, 3); (1, 2, 3, 4); (1, 2, 3, 4, 5). As you can see, this structure is constructed by adding on different movements or movement phrases.
- Call and response—This form is "conversational": one dancer moves and the other dancer(s) responds to (answers) the initial mover with movement.
- Chance dance—This is a series of dance phrases performed in a random order. Each time the dance is done, it is in a different order and therefore has a different appearance.
- Motif and development—This form involves a brief movement phrase (the motif) that is danced then developed into a full-blown dance or section of a dance. You should always be able to identify the motif within the developed movement.
- Suite—This form uses different tempos and qualities in each of its three or more sections.

Dance-Making Processes

As used in this book, the three terms we describe in this section are dance-making processes. They are methods you and your students may use to enhance a dance and carry it forward to its ultimate conclusion.

- Transition—This connects one movement or movement phrase to the next movement or movement phrase. For example, if you have a movement at a low level followed by a movement at a high level, you can insert a transitional move at the middle level (see figure 5.1).
- Contrast—This adds interest through developing opposite shapes, movements, or movement phrases. For example, if you have a shape made of angles, you then make a shape out of curves (see figure 5.2).

Figure 5.1 A linking movement can take dancers from one level to another.

Figure 5.2 Contrast in movement makes for a dynamic presentation.

Figure 5.3 One dancer can complement another, creating a total picture.

- Complementary—This involves developing different but related shapes, movements, or movement phrases. For example, if you make a shape out of curves, you make a different shape, but still of curves (see figure 5.3).

Dance-Making Elements

These are elements that organize the dancers in the dance, including

- solo, duet, trio, ensemble (the number of people dancing at one time);
- facings of dancers;
- groupings/formations;
- symmetrical (even numbers of dancers around a center line) and asymmetrical (uneven numbers of dancers around a center line) shapes and formations; and
- partnering and weight-sharing (see figure 5.4).

Dance-making elements that manipulate movement include the following:

- Unison
- Repetition
- Variety (see figure 5.5)
- Abstract
- Literal
- Levels
- Size of movement
- Changes in tempo
- Floor patterns
- Air patterns

In addition, consider adding dance-making elements through which you can guide the audience's attention, such as focal points and also silence or stillness (see figure 5.6).

Figure 5.4 Partnering and weight sharing equals trust and teamwork.

Figure 5.5 Variety adds spice to life.

Figure 5.6 The boy at the low level is the focal point.

Summary

Choose a structure to organize and support the main idea of a dance. Then use the dance-making processes to connect and clarify sections of dances. Dance-making elements keep the dancers, movement, and audience focused on the main idea. You may also use elements to fill in and embellish the main idea. Now, in part VI, we discover how special effects can further enhance and embellish your dances.

PART VI

Adding Architectural Details:
Effects That Affect Meaning

Now you have an idea for your dance and have put movements together. What are other details that will influence the structure, meaning, and overall concept of the dance? How can attention to these details make an adequate dance into something really special? In this part, we introduce you to music, costumes, props, lighting, and scenery as they relate to dance.

Music

As you know, music is an integral part of dance. Most people choose the music for their piece in the early part of the dance-making process, and, many times, the music is a primary source of inspiration. In many of the dance construction models, however, we don't stress the selection of music or how to count it out (but see part IV for a simple example). We simply suggest that the music you choose shouldn't be burdensome to work with. The students are usually adept at finding the breaks in the music. You may wish, though, to ask them to establish musical phrases (sentences), which, in turn, will guide their work.

Music can establish a mood, an atmosphere, a sense of time and place. As mentioned, music may also be the source of your inspiration. For example, Neil Diamond's "Coming to America" could drive the design of a dance about immigration. The music from *Schindler's List* could tie several dance pieces together on the subject of the Holocaust. There are many songs about weather on *Winnie the Pooh* CDs, films, or videos.

Children love to bring in music, and this opportunity can be motivating. Simply make sure that it is appropriate for school use. Establish ground rules and double-check for compliance. One guideline we find helpful is that the student must be able to honestly answer "Yes" to the question, "Can you listen to it with your mother?"

Costumes

Thinking about costumes can be daunting. You may wonder, "Where will I get the ideas and funds? Who will sew the seams?" The first rule of costumes is "Keep it simple!" The simplest idea is to pick several coordinating colors, creating a color theme. Have the students bring in and wear tops and bottoms to fit the color theme. They can borrow from one another, wear printed T-shirts inside out, sweats, or shorts. Let's say you are staging a dance about the sun. The children can wear reds and yellows with a few children wearing orange for an accent color. If the sun is part of a piece that includes the sky, those children can wear shades of blue. You may also make costume pieces out of construction or crepe paper if they are only to be worn once. Be sure, however, to have the children wear such costumes in a dress rehearsal to test for durability.

If you are on an even tighter budget, you can look in Salvation Army stores (or any resale shop) to find anything from skirts and shirts to pants and jackets. Remember, from the audience to the stage, the look is very different than from up close. You don't have to worry about a few worn spots or other problems. Such blemishes won't spoil the illusion.

Props

Using props can be an inexpensive way of dressing up your dances as well as enhancing or driving the movement. As with costumes, your or students' imagination will help you envision and then create appropriate props. Use the following examples to help get you started. For "I Feel Pretty" from *West Side Story*, make mirrors out of card stock and aluminum foil, decorating one side and gluing the foil to the other side. For "Under the Sea," cut out fish shapes in duplicate, color them brightly, staple the perimeter, and stuff them with soft paper. Mount them on dowels or simply have dancers hold them in their hands (see figure 6.1). A favorite example from *Building Dances* involves wearing a tissue box on the head. Several students wearing this prop could form the yellow brick road in the *Wizard of Oz* or the Great Wall of China. When you paint them with commonly used colors, you can reuse them. Perhaps the boxes could even be the wall in *The Hunchback of Notre Dame* that the gargoyles sit on. Become a scavenger and look at every object as a potential prop. Your school's art teacher may also be a good resource for ideas and materials.

Figure 6.1 Props enhance the story line.

Lighting

This is an area in which there is usually little room for imagination beyond what your physical facility allows. If your school has a proper auditorium, it might be equipped with strip lights overhead and at the foot of the stage. Usually, these have glass lenses that are alternately blue, red, and clear or white. Whatever you have, light the stage as well as possible so that the audience can see the dancers (see figure 6.2). If you have the funds, hire a local production company with the right experience and let them light your dances more creatively. Such companies usually produce road shows and rock shows, but they may be open to accepting a reduced rate to meet your needs.

Figure 6.2 Theatrical lighting equipment will enhance a dance or performance.

If your multipurpose room is where your students must perform, you are even more limited. For example, if you turn off the main lights to the room to create the illusion of a theater, you also turn off the lights that illuminate the performers. So in this case, consider borrowing some floodlights to light the stage area.

Many high schools have an appropriate stage and at least a minimal lighting setup. If you can take your children to the high school facilities, you might be able to work with the teacher in charge of maintaining the equipment. You might even be able to change gels (the cellophane-like material that goes in front of the light fixture to produce colored light, creating the proper atmosphere or mood for your dance). Stay flexible, and ideas will come with experience. However, always remember this rule of thumb: Seeing the dancers is better than creating a "mood," particularly when you are videotaping the performance.

Scenery

This doesn't have to be overwhelming! First, decide if you really need or want scenery. Is the scenery necessary to the dance or does it just create a mood or illusion? Does the scenery have to last one performance or a long run of a show? Do you have enough extra people to move the scenery around? Do you have a place to safely store it? Consider, too, that sometimes you have to sacrifice an elaborate scenery concept so that you can fit the dancers on the stage. To both leave space for the dancers and keep things simple, think of scenery in terms of set pieces such as a bush, a doorframe or an arch, a balcony, or a bench. Such items are also reusable in other dances in the show and in the future.

Specifically, here are some suggestions for making multiuse scenery. Start with four-by-eight-foot sheets of plywood. Make a stand to support, or brace, each piece. Parents, your high school's industrial arts teacher (and his or her students), or your school's custodian may be willing to help. You or your students can paint a "scene" on both sides of the plywood (either horizontally or vertically). When the supports come off, each piece may be stored flat against a wall. As another benefit, you may paint over the plywood many times.

If all you need is one scene for an entire show, tape huge sheets of brown paper to the back wall of the staging area. Then you or your students may paint this. At the show's end, you simply pull it down and throw it away. For example, if you are doing *Winnie the Pooh*, the backdrop could be a scene of the Hundred-Acre

Figure 6.3   A simple cardboard tree makes this story come alive.

Woods. You could "build" a tree to place center stage, then have all the activity take place around the tree (see figure 6.3). If the whole show is about New York City, you could paint a backdrop of the skyline and use set pieces for the different dances.

Summary

When it comes to adding architectural details to dances, you are limited only by your and your students' imaginations, your physical surroundings (venue), and, oh yes—money. Asking for help from your school colleagues and community at large, however, may bring your program a band of merry supporters, helping you find much-needed equipment and supplies.

PART VII

Being the Building Inspector:
Making Sure Dance Work Is Sound

As educators, we teach lessons and facilitate activities that give students skills and knowledge, a variety of experiences, and multiple opportunities to explore concepts, processes, and principles of various content areas. The students, using the skills, knowledge, and experiences gained, may then build a dance.

But how do you assess student work fairly and efficiently? In recent years, many new ways to do this vital teaching task have evolved. In this part, we examine several reliable tools you may use to document student progress toward each standard. In this way, you—and your students—may function as "building inspectors."

Ways of Assessing Student Work

How do we know if a child has learned? How many times must the child repeat the task or skill? Can he or she teach, explain, write about, and demonstrate what was learned in a variety of ways and a number of times? You should use a variety of assessment tools over an extended period of time to ensure the child has assimilated the body of learning needed to meet each standard. The following information will help you explore the various assessment tools as they pertain to dance:

- Individual projects—Students are involved in every aspect of the project from the planning stages through the assessment. Students may collect data, set goals, plan, analyze, problem-solve, and make decisions.

- Group projects—Students work together in small groups to take a theme from its inspiration through its development. The end result may take the form of a performance or classroom presentation, including visuals such as photos and videotapes.

- Journals—Students document and reflect upon specific aspects of a project or performance over time. Individuals, small groups, or a whole class may each keep a journal.

- Parental reports—Students take home forms for parents to sign as evidence of their work. For example, give students a practice log form, which helps students document date, time, and tasks completed. Parents sign and return the forms.

- Interviews—Plan a series of questions you ask students to discover what the students have learned.

- Peer observations—Students observe each other. For example, one group observes, commenting on the other group's work and competency level, either verbally or using an individual reporting form. They could then switch roles.

- Self-assessments—Each student looks at her or his growth and progress. For example, she or he uses a specific rating scale or set of criteria by which to report thoughts on a particular project or her or his work over a period of time (e.g., unit, semester, school year).

- Written tests—Formats include true or false, short answer, fill in the blanks, short essays, skills checklists, and long essays.

- Rubrics—This is a tool that uses established criteria and assigns a score to the student's work (see full discussion under next section titled "The Assessment Process").

- Portfolios—These provide a systematic way to collect and document student work. Well-designed and well-maintained portfolios are a necessary part of any assessment because they reveal the learning process as seen through completed student work. The following are types of documentation you might include in a portfolio (note that many of these encompass the assessment tools already discussed in this list):

- Student research
- Journal entries
- Worksheets (from specific lessons)
- Quizzes
- Practice logs
- Pre- and posttests (questionnaires or surveys)
- Evaluations (teacher, peer, self-, other)
- Program and various performance documentation (e.g., National Dance Standards and National Standards for Physical Education)
- Writing assignments
- Revisions of work
- Videotaped documentation of process and performance
- Audiotapes of interviews
- Class notes
- Certificates of achievement

The Assessment Process

Ideally, in the assessment process, the best results come from a combination of all the methods we've explained. This approach gives a well-rounded view of each student over time as collected and documented in the portfolio. But this is a lot to juggle. Developing forms can help make the assessment process easier. These forms may be checklists of criteria, self-evaluation forms, generic skill evaluation forms, and dance task evaluations that can be completed by peer, teacher, self, and/or an outside audience.

Criteria

Criteria are what defines the piece of work. They are the pieces of what you want to see as an end result. In short, the criteria identify important aspects of performance and define "good" qualities. If the work is being designed to meet a standard, then the criteria must address the specific content of the standard.

The following is an example of a set of criteria for a dance task in which the student or student group must create a dance:

- The dance has a clear beginning, middle, and an end.
- The dance has two locomotor movements and one nonlocomotor movement.
- The dance uses a zigzagging floor pattern.
- The dance has two focus changes.
- The dance has a tempo change.
- The dance has at least one level change.
- The dance demonstrates mastery of a specific skill, such as a turn.
- The dance is well rehearsed and is performed for others.

Rubric

As mentioned earlier, a *rubric* is a tool that uses established criteria and assigns a score to the student's work. A good rubric should be specific enough to be used by anyone and also tell students what you expect of them, regarding a particular skill or performance task. Thus, you have to determine what is acceptable (at standard), unacceptable (below standard), and what is beyond the standard (above standard.) Then you must establish a point system for each rating to obtain a rubric score. For example, you might assign a score of three points for "above standard," two points for "at standard," and one point for "below standard."

You may use the generic rubrics shown in figure 7.1 and the form on page 39 to assess and score any skill or dance task, providing you have established criteria for the skill or dance task. (*Note:* For our purposes, *skill* refers to a single move or technique, e.g., a jump. A *dance task* is a combination or integration of skills, concepts, and processes, e.g., a jump with a full turn.)

If you ask a student to perform a jump with a full turn, the criteria for this dance task might read as follows:

- Student takes off from two feet, pushing off from slightly bent knees.
- Student makes a 360-degree revolution in the air.
- The body moves as one unit and is fully stretched.
- Arms help the performer make the revolution and are in a previously established position.
- Student lands on two feet with knees slightly bent, facing the starting direction.

Armed with these criteria, you are now able to plug the information into a rubric to come up with a rating.

Generic Dance Task Rubric

3 = Above standard: Student completes all criteria of task and performs end product with a polished performance quality; creates own variation of the task; accurately identifies and analyzes all aspects of the task in writing, describing the skills, elements, and processes involved; integrates what has been learned into the dance-making; creates a dance based on the task; and develops aesthetic criteria and uses it to improve the piece.

2 = At standard: Student completes all established criteria of task; demonstrates confidence and appears comfortable performing the task; makes teacher-directed variations and/or changes within the task; names, identifies, and demonstrates dance elements and skills within the process of the task; uses the skills, elements, and processes learned in combination with another task; successfully adds conceptual information learned into own body of knowledge and integrates it into personal repertoire; and documents process of task through reflective journal entries.

1 = Below standard: Student has not met all criteria of the skill; requires more time to understand and complete the task; needs to refine performance of task; names, identifies, and demonstrates elements and skills within the task when prompted; aspects of task still in need of correction; performs some aspects of the task, however, still unable to put it all together; and cannot completely integrate elements of the task into personal repertoire.

Figure 7.1 Generic dance task rubric.

Assessment Form for Blueprint Dance

Outcome desired: Create a dance, taking it from a concept, to a flat visual (two-dimensional) image, to movement (three-dimensional space).

Criteria	Dance Standards
Dance depicts blueprint.	National Dance Content Standards 3 & 7
Dance includes movement at low, high, and middle levels.	National Dance Content Standard 2
Dance takes a two-dimensional item and turns it into a three-dimensional portrayal.	National Dance Content Standard 1
Students can read a simple blueprint.	New Standards: Applied Learning A3a
Dance uses locomotor and nonlocomotor movement.	Physical Education Standard 2
Students provide a written description of the process of making a dance from a blueprint.	New Standards: English Language Arts E2d
Portfolio shows evidence of using the seven steps of building a dance.	National Standard for Physical Education 2 National Dance Content Standard 2

Portfolio Evidence/Work

- Video of created dance
- Created blueprint
- Evidence/documentation of seven steps of building a dance, e.g., Step 1: Written description of making a dance from a blueprint
- Completed self-, teacher, and peer evaluation forms

Rubric

3 = Above standard: The dance addresses all criteria and is executed at performance-quality level. Piece is revised based on teacher, peer, and self-evaluations. Portfolio work is completed.

2 = At standard: The dance addresses all criteria and is shared with the class. Portfolio work is completed.

1 = Below standard: The dance is missing some of the criteria but is shared with the class. Portfolio work is not complete or revised.

Score: _____   Name of evaluator: _____

(check one): Teacher _____   Peer _____   Self _____

Think of this generic rubric (see figure 7.1) as a "menu" from which you may select aspects you want to score. Many times your choices should depend on the experience level of the student. For example, "above standard" for a skill performed by a 2nd grader would entail using the skill in creating a dance, while a 10th grader should be able to accurately teach the skill to a peer then analyze and correct the peer's performance where needed.

In addition, use the form on page 39 to assess the dance construction models provided in both this book and *Building Dances*.

Summary

Standards and assessment go hand in hand. Fortunately, you have several options for assessing whether student dance work has successfully met standards. Your teaching strategies and activities are the means to an end, while the resulting student work indicates student knowledge and acts as evidence that the student has met the standard(s) you were teaching toward.

PART VIII

Building More Dances From Sample Blueprints:
Dance Construction Models

PLANS

On the following pages, we provide a wealth of teaching materials. We designed these 23 dance construction models to inspire you in a variety of ways:

- You will become aware that building dances (choreography) can be a fun game, an activity that will inspire and intrigue both you and your students.

- You will find the dance construction models are a great way to begin to integrate learning across the curriculum. You can dance about anything!

- You will discover that whether or not you're a dance educator, you can achieve glowing results with applause from audiences and accolades from colleagues.

- You will find that students are eager creators—ready, willing, and capable of building dances.

- You will discover that when you work with the dance construction models, the seven steps to building a dance will keep you organized (see part IV).

- You will see that these dance construction models address standards every step of the way. The end result of each dance construction model is student work that satisfies multiple standards (see part II).

Blueprint Dance

Purpose

In this activity, students will learn to transform an idea from a concept, to two-dimensional art, to movement while learning about spatial relationships and teamwork.

Resources Needed

- Paper
- Crayons
- Colored markers

General Procedure

Divide the class into small groups of five or six. For each small group, place a large, clean piece of paper on a table or smooth floor. Place colored markers or pencils near the paper. Ask all but one student in each group to make a shape on the paper with one of the markers. Direct the last student (the "architect") to connect the shapes with a continuous line (see figure 8.1). Next, ask each student to create a movement pattern, depicting the shape he or she created on the paper. Finally, have the architect connect all the features of the "blueprint" with an additional movement pattern.

Sample Activity (K-4)

Once the blueprint is complete, encourage the children to observe what they have drawn from all angles. Choose one group to work with while the rest of the class

Figure 8.1 Blueprints make building dances fun.

observes the process. Explain that each person may make a shape or pattern with one movement or more than one movement (identify this as a "movement phrase"). Have the whole group perform each person's creation in tandem.

When all group members have completed their moves and are "frozen" in space, the last person—the architect—creates the flowing pattern that links the shapes, creating a dance from the individual pieces. Finally, have the group practice the entire dance as one, flowing piece. Circulate among groups as they work to implement the process (the demonstration group could draw a new blueprint or refine their original).

As an additional idea, consider suggesting that group members link physically with the architect as she or he travels from shape to shape.

Sample Activity (5-8)

Students this age can teach each other their individual movement patterns, and after they have completed the dance as individuals, they may all do the repeat at the same time.

As an alternative, they may also perform their individual movement patterns simultaneously, creating a chaotic effect as the architect threads through the group. Use the ABA dance-making structure to form the dance (see part V).

Sample Activity (9-12)

Students this age are capable of much more intricate shapes and patterns than younger students. You might also like to have them research what an actual blueprint looks like and what information it holds to encourage them to add details to their dances.

Use the theme and variation structure (part V): Have students build on their first inspiration, always coming back to the original shapes and blueprint. They can work off each other, one person's moves generated from another's, in pairs, and then all together after the architect connects them.

Assessment Form for Blueprint Dance

Outcome desired: Create a dance, taking it from a concept, to a flat visual (two-dimensional) image, to movement (three-dimensional space).

Criteria	Dance Standards
Dance depicts blueprint.	National Dance Content Standards 3 & 7
Dance includes movement at low, high, and middle levels.	National Dance Content Standard 2 National Standard for Physical Education 1
Dance takes a two-dimensional item and turns it into a three-dimensional portrayal.	National Dance Content Standard 1
Students can read a simple blueprint.	New Standards: Applied Learning A3a
Dance uses locomotor and nonlocomotor movement.	National Standard for Physical Education 2 National Dance Content Standard 1
Students provide a written description of the process of making a dance from a blueprint.	New Standards: English Language Arts E2d
Portfolio shows evidence of using the seven steps of building a dance.	National Standard for Physical Education 2 National Dance Content Standard 2

Portfolio Evidence/Work

- Video of created dance
- Created blueprint
- Evidence/documentation of seven steps of building a dance, e.g., Step 1: Written description of making a dance from a blueprint
- Completed self-, teacher, and peer evaluation forms

Rubric

3 = Above standard: The dance addresses all criteria and is executed at performance-quality level. Piece is revised based on teacher, peer, and self-evaluations. Portfolio work is completed.

2 = At standard: The dance addresses all criteria and is shared with the class. Portfolio work is completed.

1 = Below standard: The dance is missing some of the criteria but is shared with the class. Portfolio work is not complete or revised.

Score: _____   Name of evaluator: _____

(check one): Teacher _____   Peer _____   Self _____

Carnivale

Purpose

In this activity, students explore different festivals and how and why people all over the world create and participate in celebrations.

Resources Needed

- Reference books on various celebrations around the world
- Artwork materials (e.g., masks, decorated noise-makers, and costumes)
- Videos of various celebrations around the world

General Procedure

Choose a celebration or festival, such as Mardi Gras or Carnivale (Brazil). Students learn and/or research all they can about the event. Students create a dance based on what they've learned.

Sample Activity (K–4)

Read the story of *Winnie the Pooh.* Create a parade using the theme and characters from the story. Students may create movement signatures, which are short movement phrases or linked poses that only a specific character does. Add costumes and music. Parade through the hallways at school.

Sample Activity (5–8)

Have students research the concept of Carnivale. Working in small groups, students choose themes for their group and create ideas for a Carnivale parade. Help groups combine to put together a parade dance, using all the different themes they've developed.

Sample Activity (9–12)

Have students research the historical, social, and cultural significance of Mardi Gras. Create a series of "dance events" depicting the many facets of Mardi Gras (see figure 8.2). Perform the events as a show for an audience.

Figure 8.2 Addition of costumes makes the dance even more authentic.

Assessment Form for Carnivale

Outcome desired: Create a celebration dance.

Criteria	Dance Standards
The dance depicts the feeling of festival participants.	National Dance Content Standards 3 & 5
Researched facts are evident in dance.	New Standards: Applied Learning A3a
Dance has a clear beginning, middle, and end.	National Dance Content Standard 2
Students can explain why, where, and when celebration dances occur.	New Standards: Applied Learning A2a National Dance Content Standard 5 National Standard for Physical Education 6
Dance uses appropriate costumes and props (optional).	National Dance Content Standard 7 National Standards for Arts Education: Visual Arts 6
Portfolio shows evidence of using the seven steps of building a dance.	National Standard for Physical Education 2 National Dance Content Standard 2

Portfolio Evidence/Work

- Video of created dance
- Evidence of research, e.g., notes on various celebrations
- Evidence/documentation of seven steps of building a dance, e.g., Step 1: What celebration students chose and why
- Completed self-, teacher, and peer evaluation forms

Rubric

3 = Above standard: The dance addresses all criteria and is executed at performance-quality level. Piece is revised based on teacher, peer, and self-evaluations. Portfolio work is completed.

2 = At standard: The dance addresses all criteria and is shared with the class. Portfolio work is completed.

1 = Below standard: The dance is missing some of the criteria but is shared with the class. Portfolio work is not complete or revised.

Score: _____   Name of evaluator: _____

(check one): Teacher _____   Peer _____   Self _____

Communication Dance

Purpose

In this activity, students research how people and animals tell each other things to discover the many ways to get and receive messages.

Resources Needed

- Reference books on communication
- A chart of sign language symbols
- Computers
- Drums
- Signal flags

General Procedure

Students research how people and animals communicate in the present and how they have done so in the past. Some of the ways the students may explore include gestures, expressions (facial and body; see figure 8.3), sign language, smoke signals, flag signals (semaphore), Morse code, drumming, light beacons, and ram's horns (shofars).

Sample Activity (K-4)

Teach students the "Hello Dance" in which they say "hello" and "good-bye" in five languages, either actual or created. Next have students create a shape or signature movement for each of the languages and then link them to make a longer dance piece.

Figure 8.3   Facial expressions clarify the meaning of some movements.

Sample Activity (5-8)

Have students research selected communication methods to inspire the movement and create "conversations" between students. For example, have students study Morse code and flag signals (semaphore). One variation is to direct one group of students to "say" something in a Morse code rhythm and another group to answer with flag signals.

Sample Activity (9-12)

Have students observe people and their body language. Then have them create a dance portraying the body language they have seen.

Assessment Form for Communication Dance

Outcome desired: Create a dance that communicates a message.

Criteria	Dance Standards
The dance communicates a message.	National Dance Content Standard 3
Researched facts are evident in dance.	New Standards: Applied Learning A3a
Dance has a clear beginning, middle, and end.	National Dance Content Standard 2
Students can explain the message verbally and then nonverbally.	New Standards: Applied Learning A2a New Standards: English Language Arts E1c
Students use appropriate costumes, props, and music (optional).	National Dance Content Standard 7 National Standards for Arts Education: Visual Arts 6 National Standards for Arts Education: Music 8
Portfolio shows evidence of using the seven steps of building a dance.	National Standard for Physical Education 2 National Dance Content Standard 2

Portfolio Evidence/Work

- Video of created dance
- Evidence of research, e.g., brainstorm list of methods of communication
- Evidence/documentation of seven steps of building a dance, e.g., Step 1: Message in written form
- Completed self-, teacher, and peer evaluation forms

Rubric

3 = Above standard: The dance addresses all criteria and is executed at performance-quality level. Piece is revised based on teacher, peer, and self-evaluations. Portfolio work is completed.

2 = At standard: The dance addresses all criteria and is shared with the class. Portfolio work is completed.

1 = Below standard: The dance is missing some of the criteria but is shared with the class. Portfolio work is not complete or revised.

Score: _____   Name of evaluator: _____

(check one): Teacher _____   Peer _____   Self _____

Concepts and Basic Skills Dance

Purpose

In this activity, students explore conceptual skills as inspiration for creating movement patterns.

Resource Needed

- Classroom teacher

General Procedure

Teach students the specific, age-appropriate academic concepts and skills for their level. Then, through the medium of dance, have them explore those movement concepts and skills and create dances (see figure 8.4).

Figure 8.4   The classroom teacher is the resource for the Concepts and Basic Skills Dance.

Sample Activity (K-4)

Explore concepts and skills through movement and make dances about them— for example, opposites, vocabulary words, sentence structure or grammar, remembering details, reading comprehension, following directions, listening, finding patterns, finding similarities, duplicating, predicting outcomes, classifying, sequencing, making inferences, alphabetical order, and so on. One example would be a dance made from all the action words (verbs) in a paragraph.

Sample Activity (5-8)

Choose more complex concepts and skills than with younger students, such as fact or opinion, determining the main idea of a story, determining word meaning from context, recognizing details, analogies, abstract versus concrete, and so on. A dance example could be a motif and development dance showing a simple dance phrase and more developed dance phrases using "details."

Sample Activity (9-12)

Using elementary or middle school concepts and skills, have students create a lecture and demonstration showing their meanings through movement. Arrange for students to share the material they develop with lower grades to teach younger students.

Assessment Form for Concepts and Basic Skills Dance

Outcome desired: Create a dance based on a concept or skill.

Criteria	Dance Standards
The dance depicts the basic skills or concept.	National Dance Content Standard 3
Researched facts are evident in dance.	New Standards: Applied Learning A3a
Dance has a clear beginning, middle, and end.	National Dance Content Standard 2
Students can explain the particular concept or skill and then show it nonverbally.	New Standards: Applied Learning A2a
Dance is set to music (optional).	National Dance Content Standard 7 National Standards for Arts Education: Music 8
Portfolio shows evidence of using the seven steps of building a dance.	National Standard for Physical Education 2 National Dance Content Standard 2

Portfolio Evidence/Work

- Video of created dance
- Evidence of research, e.g., written description of the concept or skill
- Evidence/documentation of seven steps of building a dance, e.g., Step 1: Videotapes of the process of developing movement
- Completed self-, teacher, and peer evaluation forms

Rubric

3 = Above standard: The dance addresses all criteria and is executed at performance-quality level. Piece is revised based on teacher, peer, and self-evaluations. Portfolio work is completed.

2 = At standard: The dance addresses all criteria and is shared with the class. Portfolio work is completed.

1 = Below standard: The dance is missing some of the criteria but is shared with the class. Portfolio work is not complete or revised.

Score: _____ Name of evaluator: _____

(check one): Teacher _____ Peer _____ Self _____

Countries Dance

Purpose

In this activity, students create a dance based on their research of a particular country or region.

Resources Needed

- Videos of various ethnic and folk dances
- Music from various countries or regions
- Reference books about various countries or regions

General Procedure

Choose or allow small groups to choose a country or region. Have students research the country or region, then create an original dance or re-create a dance inspired from observing dances from that country or region (see figure 8.5).

Figure 8.5   You can add to your knowledge of a country by observing fashion and dress.

Sample Activity (K-4)

Show a video of a simple folk dance. Help students discuss and analyze the dance. Have them look for (1) types of movements, (2) structure, (3) formations, (4) groupings (numbers), and (5) anything else that makes it unique. Then re-create it with the children.

Sample Activity (5-8)

Have small groups study or research a country. Then direct each group to build a different dance, based on the reasons the people in that country dance (e.g., celebrations, life passages, other traditions, or just for fun).

Sample Activity (9-12)

Have students "travel" around the world through dance. Divide the class into small groups and have each group research and build a dance from a different country. Then have them compare their creations. Ask questions such as these: "How are they similar? Different?" Also encourage students to determine what circumstances inspired the dance in the country and how the movements relate to those circumstances and to the country highlighted. Perform this "world tour" for younger students.

Assessment Form for Countries Dance

Outcome desired: Create a dance based on the research of a particular country or region.

Criteria	Dance Standards
The dance reflects country or region.	National Dance Content Standards 1, 3, & 5 National Standards for History 7 (K-4)
Portfolio shows evidence of seven steps of building a dance.	National Standard for Physical Education 2 National Dance Content Standard 2
Researched facts are evident in dance.	New Standards: Applied Learning A3a
Dance has a clear beginning, middle, and end.	National Dance Content Standard 2
Students can explain the significance of the dance as it relates to the country or region.	New Standards: Applied Learning A2a National Standards for Physical Education 6 & 7
Dance is set to music of the country or region.	National Dance Content Standard 7 National Standards for Arts Education: Music 8
Dance was accurately re-created from the video.	National Dance Content Standard 4

Portfolio Evidence/Work

- Video of created dance
- Evidence of research, e.g., written description of country
- Evidence/documentation of seven steps of building a dance, e.g., Step 3: List of appropriate music that can be used from chosen country
- Completed self-, teacher, and peer evaluation forms

Rubric

3 = Above standard: The dance addresses all criteria and is executed at performance-quality level. Piece is revised based on teacher, peer, and self-evaluations. Portfolio work is completed.

2 = At standard: The dance addresses all criteria and is shared with the class. Portfolio work is completed.

1 = Below standard: The dance is missing some of the criteria but is shared with the class. Portfolio work is not complete or revised.

Score: _____ Name of evaluator: _____

(check one): Teacher _____ Peer _____ Self _____

Create-a-Line Dance

Purpose

In this activity, your students will learn how to take line dancing to a new level by requiring students to invent movements and create movement patterns, then incorporate these to fit a piece of music.

Resources Needed

- A variety of music recordings
- Videos and books about line dances
- More Deal-a-Dance cards

General Procedure

Discuss with the class the key elements of a line dance, including the fact that line dances are composed of a series of steps that usually (1) take four sets of eight counts to complete and (2) on the last count of the fourth set, the dancer turns a quarter turn to the next direction. Then the dancers repeat the entire four sets of eight counts.

Next, guide students in brainstorming themes for line dances and exploring movements and steps to carry out the theme. Have students bring in music that suits the theme they want to communicate. Decide on steps and develop a sequence for these steps to fit the music (see figure 8.6). If students cannot think of any steps to do, have them use More Deal-a-Dance cards for inspiration.

Sample Activity (K-4)

Help students choose a favorite story and design a line dance about it. Discuss the characteristics of each of the main characters. Have the students choose four characters, and create an eight-count signature movement for each. Decide on a sequence. (Remember, the last movement of the sequence must include a quarter turn.) Let the children choose a song with a 4/4 count from any appropriate recording.

Sample Activity (5-8)

Have students choose a holiday, such as Halloween, as their inspiration. Help students brainstorm types of costumes they could wear (e.g., ghosts, goblins, monsters, witches, pumpkins, and so on). Write each item on the brainstorming list on a separate index card and put them all in a box.

Divide the class into small groups. Have each group pull four cards out of the box. Then direct groups to create an eight-count locomotor movement pattern for each card, representing the character each card lists. Next, have groups develop a line dance by putting the four movement patterns together and using music to complement the dance (e.g., "The Monster Mash," "Casper, the Friendly Ghost," or "Ding, Dong, the Witch Is Dead"). Possible extensions include the following: (1) Have each group teach the other groups its dance. (2) Have students design and construct costumes in which to do their dances for an audience.

Figure 8.6 Explore different ways of building a line dance.

Sample Activity (9-12)

Play up the fact that high school students are full of school spirit. It will be easy to persuade them to create a line dance to a school pep song that happens to have a 4/4 count, lending itself to this type of dance-making. Their line dancing could also include "cheers." They could volunteer to perform at games and pep rallies. Imagine an entire student body performing in unison on the football field at halftime!

Assessment Form for Create-a-Line Dance

Outcome desired: Create a line dance based on student-invented movements and patterns.

Criteria	Dance Standards
Dance uses student-created moves and patterns.	National Dance Content Standard 1
Portfolio shows evidence of seven steps of building a dance.	National Standard for Physical Education 2 National Dance Content Standard 2
Researched facts are evident in dance.	New Standards: Applied Learning A3a
Dance has a clear beginning, middle, and end.	National Dance Content Standard 2
Students can explain the idea(s) that sparked the new movements.	New Standards: Applied Learning A2a National Standard for Physical Education 7
Dance is set to music.	National Dance Content Standard 7 National Standards for Arts Education: Music 8

Portfolio Evidence/Work

- Video of created dance
- Evidence of research, e.g., list of different line dances, analysis of what makes a line dance
- Evidence/documentation of seven steps of building a dance, e.g., Step 5: Video of phrase to be repeated
- Completed self-, teacher, and peer evaluation forms

Rubric

3 = Above standard: The dance addresses all criteria and is executed at performance-quality level. Piece is revised based on teacher, peer, and self-evaluations. Portfolio work is completed.

2 = At standard: The dance addresses all criteria and is shared with the class. Portfolio work is completed.

1 = Below standard: The dance is missing some of the criteria but is shared with the class. Portfolio work is not complete or revised.

Score: _____ Name of evaluator: _____

(check one): Teacher _____ Peer _____ Self _____

Dance-a-Quote

Purpose

In this activity, students will become more familiar with famous quotes and will explore the meaning of the quotes, within the context of the time period and speaker.

Resource Needed

- Books of quotations

General Procedure

Help students brainstorm quotes they remember. Then have them research famous people and what they have said that has had a lasting impact on society. Encourage students to embrace the whole quote and its meaning—not just the individual words—and come up with movement problems to solve. Then have them create small movement phrases to bring the quote to life.

Sample Activity (K-4)

Have students choose a quote, such as the following, from a list or come up with their own:

- "I'm feeling a little 11 o'clockish." —Winnie the Pooh
- "I'm feeling curiouser and curiouser." —Alice in Wonderland
- "If at first you don't succeed, try and try again." —W.E. Hickson

Together, teacher and students explore the meaning of the quote and why the person or character may have said it. Research where the quote first appeared. Find out what was happening at the time it was said. Together, the teacher and students devise a movement problem (a question or problem that is solved by moving), using one of the words from the quote. Teachers can guide students to enlarge that to become a movement phrase that incorporates the message of the entire quote (see figure 8.7).

Figure 8.7 Familiar quotes can lead to confident and creative movement makers.

Sample Activity (5-8)

Have students choose a quote, such as the following, from a list or come up with their own:

- "Good fences make good neighbors." —Robert Frost
- "That's one small step for [a] man, one giant leap for mankind." —Neil Armstrong
- "It's far easier to start something than it is to finish it." —Amelia Earhart

As with younger students, choose one of the quotes or one from subject matter in the core curriculum. Discuss its meaning within the time period and place. Discuss who the speaker or writer is or was. Now build a character through dance and movement personifying the speaker or author. Have several quoted characters relate to each other through dance, building a longer, more intricate dance piece.

Sample Activity (9-12)

Have students choose a quote, such as the following, from a list or come up with their own:

- "We must honor our ancestors." —Alex Haley
- "If I am not for myself, who will be?" —Pirke Avoth (second century)
- "Give a man a fish and you feed him for a day. Teach a man to fish and you feed him for a lifetime." —Chinese proverb

These three and similar quotes delve deeper into the human condition than those suggested for younger students. Have students research the basis for the quotes, develop written material (such as essays, reports, poems, or outlines), devise and solve movement problems related to the subjects, and, finally, build a dance or dances conveying the messages.

Assessment Form for Dance-a-Quote

Outcome desired: Create a dance based on a quote or a series of quotes.

Criteria	Dance Standards
The dance depicts the meaning of the quote and the character of the person making the statement.	National Dance Content Standard 3 New Standards: English Language Arts E1c
Portfolio shows evidence of seven steps of building a dance.	National Standard for Physical Education 2 National Dance Content Standard 2
Researched facts are evident in dance.	New Standards: Applied Learning A3a
Dance has a clear beginning, middle, and end.	National Dance Content Standard 2
Students can explain the meaning of the quote and the nonverbal depicts the verbal.	New Standards: Applied Learning A2a National Standard for Physical Education 7
Dance is set to music (optional).	National Dance Content Standard 7 National Standards for Arts Education: Music 8

Portfolio Evidence/Work

- Video of created dance
- Evidence of research, e.g., brainstorm a list of possible quotes
- Evidence/documentation of seven steps of building a dance, e.g., Step 6: A list of suggestions for costumes or props to help portray the quote
- Completed self-, teacher, and peer evaluation forms

Rubric

3 = Above standard: The dance addresses all criteria and is executed at performance-quality level. Piece is revised based on teacher, peer, and self-evaluations. Portfolio work is completed.

2 = At standard: The dance addresses all criteria and is shared with the class. Portfolio work is completed.

1 = Below standard: The dance is missing some of the criteria but is shared with the class. Portfolio work is not complete or revised.

Score: _____   Name of evaluator: _____

(check one): Teacher _____   Peer _____   Self _____

Dance-a-Warm-Up

Purpose

In this activity, students will learn about the content and value of a proper warm-up before physical activity. Students will also learn they may invent their own comprehensive warm-ups and share them with others. This approach motivates eager, willing participation, because designing warm-ups will start students' creative juices flowing and is an effective beginning to dance-making, which leads to excellent classroom experiences.

Resources Needed

- Charts of the circulatory system
- Heart monitors
- Thera-Bands
- Videos of various types of warm-ups (e.g., sport teams, dance companies, tai chi)
- More Deal-a-Dance cards (see page 116)

General Procedure

Discuss why a safe and proper warm-up is necessary for all physical activity as it improves performance, prevents injury, and starts the fun. The key characteristics of a safe and helpful warm-up are that is should (1) be gradual, starting slowly and building up to activity-level intensity; (2) last 5 to 10 minutes; and (3) be specific to the muscles students will use during the main activity. Draw upon students' prior knowledge of why they should warm up and previous experiences of what movements make their bodies feel loose and limber.

Discuss which types of physical activities loosen which body parts. Show videos of various warm-ups. Discuss what a progressive warm-up is, that is, top of body to bottom of body, or big muscles to smaller muscles, or the reverse.

Sample Activity (K-4)

Describe a muscle as a piece of silly putty: when you pull a cold piece it will snap quickly, but if you work it gently until it is warm you can stretch and shape it. Now introduce a specific warm-up routine. Have students stand in a circle or in lines facing you. Starting with the head, students make a figure eight going from side to side with a slight rolling motion. Lower the chin to the chest, roll the head to the right shoulder, lift the chin, and begin to roll the head back to the center. Lower the chin again, but roll to the left shoulder this time, creating a lazy figure eight. Direct students to take the movement into their shoulders, eventually including their arms. Bending and twisting at the waist, continue the figure-eight movement. Standing erect, use the feet and ankles in the same motion (one at a time). Lastly, use the legs in a similar movement.

Ask the children to combine, change the sequence of, and vary the movements just executed, then add music. Each child will have developed a movement phrase or a short dance.

Sample Activity (5-8)

Choose one section of the body that you will concentrate on, such as the hip, knee, and ankle of each leg, in turn. Ask students to think of ways to move that make those body parts seem warmer. For example, they might choose to raise the leg from the knee and replace it onto the floor. Ask students to add an ankle move (e.g., flex and point) before replacing the foot on the floor. Then, in this example, you should explore ways of shifting weight from one leg to another. Change levels (e.g., from standing onto the stomach) and alter each movement to fit the position. Make the movement locomotor when changing sides, prancing.

As with younger children, ask students to combine, change the sequence of, and vary the movements just executed, then add music. Each student will have developed a movement phrase or a short dance.

Sample Activity (9-12)

Create a "cheer" using warm-up exercises. First have students write a rap-type lyric, explaining the value of a proper warm-up and the possible consequences of not warming up. Individual groups can perform their own cheer and have a competition. They can also take the cheers to recreation centers and younger classes to help teach about warm-ups (see figure 8.8).

Figure 8.8   Cheering is not always about ball games.

Assessment Form for Dance-a-Warm-Up

Outcome desired: Create a dance based on proper warm-up methods and skills.

Criteria	Dance Standards
The dance has the components of a proper warm-up.	National Dance Content Standards 1 & 3
Portfolio shows evidence of seven steps of building a dance.	National Standard for Physical Education 2 National Dance Content Standard 2
Researched facts are evident in dance.	New Standards: Applied Learning A3a
Dance has a clear beginning, middle, and end.	National Dance Content Standard 2
Students explain why a warm-up is needed before physical activity and what movements comprise a proper warm-up.	New Standards: Applied Learning A2a National Dance Content Standard 6 National Standard for Physical Education 4
Dance is set to music (optional).	National Dance Content Standard 7 National Standards for Arts Education: Music 8

Portfolio Evidence/Work

- Video of created dance
- Evidence of research, e.g., a written explanation of why we warm up and what areas are of primary focus
- Evidence/documentation of seven steps of building a dance, e.g., Step 2: A videotape of a created movement that warms up a specific body part
- Completed self-, teacher, and peer evaluation forms

Rubric

3 = Above standard: The dance addresses all criteria and is executed at performance-quality level. Piece is revised based on teacher, peer, and self-evaluations. Portfolio work is completed.

2 = At standard: The dance addresses all criteria and is shared with the class. Portfolio work is completed.

1 = Below standard: The dance is missing some of the criteria but is shared with the class. Portfolio work is not complete or revised.

Score: _____ Name of evaluator: _____

(check one): Teacher _____ Peer _____ Self _____

Dance Is in the Bag

Purpose

In this activity, students will develop verbal and storytelling skills to help them create dances, thereby building self-confidence and interpersonal communication skills.

Resources Needed

Please see Sample Activity descriptions for quantities.

- Paper bags
- Assortment of everyday items

General Procedure

Give each group or student a bag with items hidden in it. Then have students do the following: (1) Without looking, pull one item from your bag. Start a story about that item. (2) Pull a second item out and continue your story adding the second item into your story. (3) Pull the third item from the bag and finish your story, including that item.

After groups or students have developed their stories, direct them to develop movement patterns and phrases that link the items into a dance version, retelling their story (see figure 8.9).

Figure 8.9 Surprises spark creativity.

Sample Activity (K-4)

At this age, students will likely need to do this activity as a whole class under your direct guidance. Fill one or more bags ahead of time with three items each, then select one child to open a bag and start the story. For example, the student pulls out a rubber worm. He starts the story with, "This is a good worm that crawls through the earth in a garden." You may opt to let him continue longer about the worm or let another child take over and pull out the second item, such as a flower. She may say, "The beautiful blue flower is afraid that the worm will eat her." Again, you may let this child continue further about the flower or select a third child to pull the third item from the bag, such as a picture of a vase. He might say, "A little girl came along and picked the flower. She put it into the vase with fresh water so that it was saved from the worm. The worm was really disappointed to lose the beautiful flower."

Have other students help repeat the story and brainstorm movements that may help retell the story. Then help the class retell the story completely through movement. Find ways to involve every student in moving. For example, add a person to be the little girl who picks the flower and a person to be the water. In addition, divide the class into groups of "items," that is, each fifth of the class can be one of the items (the three items from the bag, the girl, and the water). This will keep everyone moving and learning.

Sample Activity (5-8)

Students in these grades should be able to do this activity more independently than in the earlier grades. Divide students into pairs or small groups. Let students fill the bags as they see fit with three items per bag, from a variety of items you supply. If you like, several bags may be filled the same way or differently. You can trade off the "fillers" and "tellers" of the story within or between pairs or groups. Finally, have the pairs or small groups develop movements to retell their stories.

Sample Activity (9-12)

Provide three "issue" items from newspaper and magazine articles (e.g., about drug abuse, cigarettes, teen pregnancy, or what easy access to weapons does to a community). Either prefill or have students fill the bags. We have found that if the teacher loads the bags, the students are more free to deal with how they feel about the issues. You will also find that when they put their feelings into movement, they get to the core of the issues more easily. Add music; students at this level will have definite ideas on the music that "speaks" to the particular issue.

Assessment Form for Dance Is in the Bag

Outcome desired: Create a dance based on a story that is made up by using the contents of a bag

Criteria	Dance Standards
Dance depicts the created story.	National Dance Content Standards 1 & 3 New Standards: English Language Arts E1c
Portfolio shows evidence of seven steps of building a dance.	National Standard for Physical Education 2 National Dance Content Standard 2
Researched facts are evident in dance.	New Standards: Applied Learning A3a
Dance has a clear beginning, middle, and end.	National Dance Content Standard 2
Students write the story then tell the story, verbally, then dance it.	New Standards: Applied Learning A2a National Standard for Physical Education 7
The movement signatures truly represent the items.	National Dance Content Standards 1, 3, & 4 National Standards for Physical Education 1 & 7
The story line makes use of the items from the bag.	National Dance Content Standards 1 & 3 New Standards: English Language Arts E1c
Dance is set to music (optional).	National Dance Content Standard 7 National Standards for Arts Education: Music 8

Portfolio Evidence/Work

- Video of created dance
- Evidence of research, e.g., audio- or videotaped discussion of what each item represents
- Evidence/documentation of seven steps of building a dance, e.g., Step 4: Videotape movement signatures for each item chosen
- Completed self-, teacher, and peer evaluation forms

Rubric

3 = Above standard: The dance addresses all criteria and is executed at performance-quality level. Piece is revised based on teacher, peer, and self-evaluations. Portfolio work is completed.

2 = At standard: The dance addresses all criteria and is shared with the class. Portfolio work is completed.

1 = Below standard: The dance is missing some of the criteria but is shared with the class. Portfolio work is not complete or revised.

Score: _____ Name of evaluator: _____

(check one): Teacher _____ Peer _____ Self _____

Purpose

In this activity, dance helps students explore people, places, and events throughout history by using knowledge of history as inspiration for creating dances. (*Note:* Anthropologists and dance historians have researched and explored that dance in one form or another has existed since the Stone Age as evidenced by cave etchings. Both the music and the artwork of the time and place give us information about what was happening in the world [see figure 8.10].)

CAVE DRAWINGS

ASIAN DANCE

MEDITERRANEAN DANCE

COURT DANCE

DANCE AS ENTERTAINMENT

Figure 8.10 Both the music and the artwork of the time and place give us information.

Resources Needed

- History reference books
- Library and museum exhibits about specific events in history
- Picture book collections on various related subjects
- Literature based on a time in history, such as historical fiction
- A classroom teacher to work with
- Music that depicts the time in history, such as Renaissance, baroque, bebop, or swing

General Procedure

Choose an important event, person, or place. Research the subject matter. Report on it, and then create a dance based on the subject.

Sample Activity (K-4)

A classroom teacher helps students as a group research all the aspects of the Plymouth Rock landing. Next guide them to develop dance movements that depict each aspect of the landing. Then have them write a short story about the landing. Finally, help them re-create the story through dance.

Sample Activity (5-8)

Have individuals or small groups research Thomas Edison and the invention of the electric lightbulb. Then direct each individual or group to create a dance based on the lightbulb itself, how it works, Thomas Edison and his reaction to his invention, and how the invention has and still impacts the world. (As an alternative, have each student or group select their own invention and its inventor to research and dance about.)

Sample Activity (9-12)

Have students research the atomic bomb and fusion or another controversial historical event. Direct them to explore how the subject and its impact on society are viewed and how it feels to them. Finally, have them put these feelings into movement phrases to create dances.

Assessment Form for Dance Through History

Outcome desired: Create a dance based on a specific event in history.

Criteria	Dance Standards
The dance depicts the particular event.	National Dance Content Standards 3, 5, & 7
Portfolio shows evidence of seven steps of building a dance.	National Standard for Physical Education 2 National Dance Content Standard 2
Researched facts are evident in dance.	New Standards: Applied Learning A3a
Dance has a clear beginning, middle, and end.	National Dance Content Standard 2
Students can clearly explain the event they have explored.	New Standards: Applied Learning A2a National Standards for History (depends on topic)
Dance is set to music.	National Dance Content Standard 7 National Standards for Arts Education: Music 8

Portfolio Evidence/Work

- Video of created dance
- Evidence of research, e.g., research notes concerning the event in history
- Evidence/documentation of seven steps of building a dance, e.g., Step 5: Videotape different ways of combining a series of movements
- Completed self-, teacher, and peer evaluation forms

Rubric

3 = Above standard: The dance addresses all criteria and is executed at performance-quality level. Piece is revised based on teacher, peer, and self-evaluations. Portfolio work is completed.

2 = At standard: The dance addresses all criteria and is shared with the class. Portfolio work is completed.

1 = Below standard: The dance is missing some of the criteria but is shared with the class. Portfolio work is not complete or revised.

Score: _____ Name of evaluator: _____

(check one): Teacher _____   Peer _____   Self _____

Dance Through Time

Purpose

In this activity, students explore a time period in history and create dances based on facts that they have learned about that time period, helping them gain a sense of why and how people might have danced as well as get a glimpse of how people functioned in another era.

Resources Needed

- History books
- Videos of vernacular dances
- Movies portraying different time periods
- Interviews with older people
- Trips to museums
- A classroom teacher to work with
- Music from the time period

General Procedure

Choose an era or decade. Have or help students research the time period through interviewing, watching films or videos, traditional library research, and studying artwork from books depicting the era. Then have groups create dances based on some aspect of the time period (see figure 8.11).

Figure 8.11 Every decade had their own dances. It's fun to learn the dances of our parents, grandparents, and ancestors.

Sample Activity (K-4)

"Visit" the 15th century by having the children observe the painting of Brueghler's children's games. (There are many collections of Brueghler's paintings in bookstores.) Guide them to create a group dance from these observations, working to depict the small vignette groupings in the painting.

Sample Activity (5-8)

Choose a specific time and place. In this example, we use the late 1800s in the southeastern United States. Students research the dance called the "Cakewalk" and write a report about the historical significance of this dance. Then have groups re-create and perform the dance.

Sample Activity (9-12)

Choose a time period and event, such as the 1940s and World War II. Have individuals or small groups each create a dance based on the mood and activities of the time and event.

Assessment Form for Dance Through Time

Outcome desired: People danced for different reasons in different time periods. Create a dance based on one of these times.

Criteria	Dance Standards
The dance accurately depicts the time period.	National Standards for Physical Education 6 & 7 National Dance Content Standards 3 & 5
Portfolio shows evidence of seven steps of building a dance.	National Standard for Physical Education 2 National Dance Content Standard 2
Researched facts are evident in dance.	New Standards: Applied Learning A3a
Dance has a clear beginning, middle, and end.	National Dance Content Standard 2
Students can explain what was going on in the world during that time period and then dance it.	New Standards: Applied Learning A2a
Dance is set to music.	National Dance Content Standard 7 National Standards for Arts Education: Music 8

Portfolio Evidence/Work

- Video of created dance
- Evidence of research, e.g., pictures of the time period
- Evidence/documentation of seven steps of building a dance, e.g., Step 1: Written or audiotaped discussion of the time period and why it was chosen
- Completed self-, teacher, and peer evaluation forms

Rubric

3 = Above standard: The dance addresses all criteria and is executed at performance-quality level. Piece is revised based on teacher, peer, and self-evaluations. Portfolio work is completed.

2 = At standard: The dance addresses all criteria and is shared with the class. Portfolio work is completed.

1 = Below standard: The dance is missing some of the criteria but is shared with the class. Portfolio work is not complete or revised.

Score: _____ Name of evaluator: _____

(check one): Teacher _____ Peer _____ Self _____

Dancing at the Joint

Purpose

In this activity, students learn more about the types of movements possible in the different joints, increasing their understanding of the terms *range of motion* and *efficiency of movement*.

Resources Needed

- Age-appropriate handouts of diagrams of the human skeleton and types of joints (one per group)
- Model skeleton
- Eyewitness video: *Skeleton*
- Magic School Bus video: *Magic School Bus Flexes Its Muscles*

General Procedure

Help students identify which types of movements are possible in each type of joint by doing a warm-up focused on different body joints (see Sample Activity [K-4]). Use the resources listed to help students relate the movements discovered in the warm-up to each type of joint and its location(s) in the body. Then direct them to create small dance phrases moving each type of joint. Put them together to build a dance called, "Dancing at the Joint" (see figure 8.12).

The main types of joints are pivot (top of neck), gliding (wrist), ball and socket (hip), hinge (knee), and saddle (thumb).

Figure 8.12   Dancing at the Joint.

Sample Activity (K-4)

Do a joint survey warm-up to identify all the possible movements at each major joint. For example, ask, "How can we move our shoulders? Our ankles and wrists? Our knees and elbows?" Next, direct small groups to make up and memorize small sequences of movements possible in the different types of joints. Then put a performance together by organizing which group goes first, second, and so on.

As a whole class, create a "finale" dance phrase (performed at the end of the dance) or a "chorus" dance phrase (performed between groups' phrases), by taking one movement from each group and putting these movements together in a new phrase. Set to music and have students perform.

Sample Activity (5-8)

As with younger students, do a joint survey warm-up to identify the types of joints and possible movements; however, this time teach the specific related vocabulary. For example, students can learn which joints can make the following moves: flexion, extension, hyperextension, lateral flexion, internal rotation, external rotation, circumduction, adduction, abduction, inversion, eversion, elevation, and depression.

In small groups or as a class, create a flexion-extension (hyperextension) phrase, an internal-external rotation and circumduction phrase, an adduction-abduction phrase, or any combination of joint movements, using as many joints in the body as possible. Combine phrases to build a dance. Set to music and have students perform.

Sample Activity (9-12)

As in the younger grades, do a joint survey warm-up, having students identify which movements are possible at each major joint; however, help students locate these joints on a skeleton chart or model, integrating the vocabulary listed in Sample Activity (5-8).

Then direct students to practice isolating these movements and identifying which dance and/or sport movements rely mainly on each type of joint movement. Together, analyze specific dance and/or sport movements for the types of joint movement needed for efficient performance. Have small groups or individuals build dance phrases that develop the small, separate isolations into fully integrated dance and/or sport movements. For example, a hurdler's leap flexes the hip and extends the knee of the front leg and externally rotates the hip and flexes the knee of the back leg. Do these movements separately; then, perhaps by using accumulation (part V), students combine the isolations into a single complete movement. Have students organize and combine these dance phrases to build a dance. Set to music and have students perform.

Assessment Form for Dancing at the Joint

Outcome desired: Create a dance that will increase range of motion and efficiency of movement.

Criteria	Dance Standards
Dance demonstrates types of movement possible in particular joints.	National Dance Content Standards 1 & 4 National Standards for Physical Education 1 & 2
Portfolio shows evidence of seven steps of building a dance.	National Standard for Physical Education 2 National Dance Content Standard 2
Researched facts are evident in dance.	New Standards: Applied Learning A3a
Dance has a clear beginning, middle, and end.	National Dance Content Standard 2
Students can name the types of joints and the movements possible in each type.	New Standards: Applied Learning A2a National Dance Content Standards 6 & 7
The student performed the types of joint movement clearly, efficiently, and accurately.	National Dance Content Standard 1 National Standard for Physical Education 1
Dance is set to music (optional).	National Dance Content Standard 7 National Standards for Arts Education: Music 8
Students demonstrate good teamwork.	National Standards for Physical Education 5 & 7
The student performed with appropriate energy and self-confidence (evidence of good rehearsal, etiquette, and work habits).	National Dance Content Standard 1 National Standard for Physical Education 1

Portfolio Evidence/Work

- Video of created dance
- Evidence of research, e.g., list of joints and their definitions
- Evidence/documentation of seven steps of building a dance, e.g., Step 2: Identify a joint and videotape an exploration of how you can manipulate that joint
- Completed self-, teacher, and peer evaluation forms

Rubric

3 = Above standard: The dance addresses all criteria and is executed at performance-quality level. Piece is revised based on teacher, peer, and self-evaluations. Portfolio work is completed.

2 = At standard: The dance addresses all criteria and is shared with the class. Portfolio work is completed.

1 = Below standard: The dance is missing some of the criteria but is shared with the class. Portfolio work is not complete or revised.

Score: _____ Name of evaluator: _____

(check one): Teacher _____ Peer _____ Self _____

Field Trip Dance

Purpose

In this activity, students will hone their observation skills through being encouraged to describe and interpret what they see.

Resources Needed

- Field trips to assorted locations, real or virtual

General Procedure

Take a real or an imaginary field trip to somewhere ordinary or exotic. For example, we can't all hop a plane to Bermuda, but we can research all aspects of making such a trip, from contacting travel agencies and airlines to chambers of commerce and tourist bureaus. A trip may take a day, a week, or however long you need to cover the material. Ultimately, you and your students build a dance that describes and interprets the place visited (see figure 8.13).

Figure 8.13   "What big teeth you have!"

Sample Activity (K-4)

Take the children to an aquarium to observe sea life. Brainstorm a master list of their observations. Then let students decide which and how many of the things they saw inspire them to create signature movements of or patterns about sea life. If desired, help them link these to create a longer movement piece or a small dance with a beginning, a middle, and an end.

Sample Activity (5-8)

Take students to the airport. Help them observe the many jobs and activities that take place there. After the trip, have them create a dance, based on their observations. For example, they may depict the people who guide the planes to the gate. They may also build a bigger, more intricate dance piece using more people and more aspects of an airport and air travel.

Sample Activity (9-12)

Let students explore a shopping mall. Then brainstorm as a class the dynamics of the stores and the people who shop in each. Are they sending signals and messages? Have small groups or individuals create movement phrases depicting shoppers and store fronts. Help students connect these phrases to make a piece called "Dancin' at the Mall."

Assessment Form for Field Trip Dance

Outcome desired: Create a dance based on a real or an imaginary field trip.

Criteria	Dance Standards
The dance depicts the place that was visited as part of the field trip.	National Dance Content Standard 3
Portfolio shows evidence of seven steps of building a dance.	National Standard for Physical Education 2 National Dance Content Standard 2
Facts researched or observed are evident in dance.	New Standards: Applied Learning A3a
Dance has a clear beginning, middle, and end.	National Dance Content Standard 2
Students write a narrative based on the place they have visited.	New Standards: English Language Arts E2c
Dance is set to music (optional).	National Dance Content Standard 7 National Standards for Arts Education: Music 8

Portfolio Evidence/Work

- Video of created dance
- Evidence of research, e.g., copies of brochures of possible field trips
- Evidence/documentation of seven steps of building a dance, e.g., Step 5: Do a practice log on time allotted for rehearsal of dance
- Completed self-, teacher, and peer evaluation forms

Rubric

3 = Above standard: The dance addresses all criteria and is executed at performance-quality level. Piece is revised based on teacher, peer, and self-evaluations. Portfolio work is completed.

2 = At standard: The dance addresses all criteria and is shared with the class. Portfolio work is completed.

1 = Below standard: The dance is missing some of the criteria but is shared with the class. Portfolio work is not complete or revised.

Score: _____   Name of evaluator: _____

(check one): Teacher _____   Peer _____   Self _____

Have a Healthy Heart Dance

Purpose

In this activity, students will create a series of dances that, when performed together, create a complete aerobic workout.

Resources Needed

- A selection of music in a variety of tempos (4/4 time works best)
- A heart rate monitor (optional)
- A watch or clock with a second hand (optional)

General Procedure

This is a complete workout with three sections: (1) Warm-up dances should start slowly, working muscles and joints for each part of the body and gradually increasing intensity to generate adequate blood flow. (2) The elevated heart rate section's dances should combine fast, continuous movements. (3) Last, but as important as the first two sections, cool-down dances should allow the heart rate to decrease gradually until the body is at rest. The following lists one format for creating a healthy heart dance:

1. Select music and use the counting method of organizing music (page 21).
2. Have students select or create movements they enjoy, using the full range of motion and following the main idea of the music.

   a. Warm-up (10 minutes)—Slow to medium tempo, using two or three selections of music for variety
   b. Elevated heart rate (20 minutes)—Fast tempo for prolonged elevation of the heart rate, using four or five selections of music for variety
   c. Cool-down (10 minutes)—Medium to slow tempo for cool-down, using two or three selections of music for variety

3. Combine movements to match the various thematic structures of the music. For example, during theme A (four 8 counts, or 32 counts), combine the following as part of the warm-up:

   a. First eight—Roll shoulders back four times (two counts each).
   b. Second eight—Circle right arm four counts and circle left arm four counts.
   c. Third eight—Repeat shoulder rolls.
   d. Fourth eight—Repeat arm circles.

4. Create a combination for theme B and for theme C. These combinations should concentrate on other joints and can be part of an extended warm-up or the beginning of the elevated heart rate section.
5. If there are introductory or transitional sections, design these so you may attach them to one of the three sections of the healthy heart dance.
6. Put all the sections together for a complete dance that encourages a healthy heart through fun exercise (see figure 8.14).

Sample Activity (K-4)

Choose music the children can identify with and enjoy. Have students select or create movements covering a wide range of motion. Put the selected movements to each piece of music. Have the children check their heart rates and feel their hearts beating at intervals throughout the three sections of dances.

Sample Activity (5-8)

Divide the class into three groups. Have each group work on one of the three workout sections of dances. Allow the children to select the music. Direct students, armed with correct information (see General Procedure), to invent movements that suit the music and the criteria for the section they are creating.

Figure 8.14   Dance for a healthy heart.

When each group finishes their dance, allow them to teach it to the other two groups, then link them to create an aerobic workout.

Sample Activity (9-12)

Assign or have the students form three groups. Continue as with fifth to eighth graders, but also have students add a chant or rap to the music, repeating the words while moving. Explain that this elevates the heart rate even more. Finish as with younger grades to create a linked and complete aerobic workout.

Assessment Form for Have a Healthy Heart Dance

Outcome desired: Construct a series of dances that, when performed together, create a complete aerobic workout.

Criteria	Dance Standards
The dances include warm-up, heart rate elevation, and cool-down.	National Dance Content Standard 2 National Standard for Physical Education 1
Portfolio shows evidence of seven steps of building a dance.	National Standard for Physical Education 2 National Dance Content Standard 2
Researched facts are evident in dance.	New Standards: Applied Learning A3a
Dance has a clear beginning, middle, and end.	National Dance Content Standard 2
Students explain the importance of an aerobic workout and how to construct one.	New Standards: Applied Learning A2a
The series of dances produced give a total workout.	National Dance Content Standards 1 & 6 National Standard for Physical Education 4
Dance is set to music.	National Dance Content Standard 7 National Standards for Arts Education: Music 8
Dances follow safe exercise practices.	National Dance Content Standards 6 & 7 National Health Education Standards 5, 6, & 7

Portfolio Evidence/Work

- Video of created dance
- Evidence of research, e.g., copy of heart rate chart
- Evidence/documentation of seven steps of building a dance, e.g., Step 3: Variety of music for workout
- Completed self-, teacher, and peer evaluation forms

Rubric

3 = Above standard: The dance addresses all criteria and is executed at performance-quality level. Piece is revised based on teacher, peer, and self-evaluations. Portfolio work is completed.

2 = At standard: The dance addresses all criteria and is shared with the class. Portfolio work is completed.

1 = Below standard: The dance is missing some of the criteria but is shared with the class. Portfolio work is not complete or revised.

Score: _____ Name of evaluator: _____

(check one): Teacher _____ Peer _____ Self _____

Map-a-Dance

Purpose

In this activity, students use maps as sources of inspiration for creating dances. Maps and trails determine pathways for movement patterns. This process encourages teamwork, enhances problem solving, and stimulates creativity.

Resources Needed

- Maps (from history books, geography books, the Internet, and/or vacation guides; also, if appropriate, science information books)
- Music appropriate for selected maps (such as "Night on Bald Mountain" for a hill and dale scenario, "Under the Sea" for a snorkeling map, or a Mickey Hart drum selection for a trip through the blood system)

Note: Maps may be real, fictional, or creations of the group or other class members.

General Procedure

Instruct students to research several maps that interest them. Next, have the students, working in small groups, select a map, chart, or trail (see figure 8.15). Then have each group create movement patterns following its chosen route.

Figure 8.15   *"Keep heading north by northwest!"*

Sample Activity (K-4)

In this example, students are studying American geography. To create a related dance, a group selects, for example, the Mohawk Trail. (*Note:* A guide to this particular trail is supplied by the Mohawk Trail Association. They can be contacted by phone at 413-743-8127, or visit their web site at **www.mohawktrail.com**.)

Have the group research the location of the trail and its history and importance during Colonial times and now. After studying the map, discuss questions such as the following with students:

- Who traveled the trail?
- How did people travel the trail?
- How long did it take to travel the entire trail?
- Where were the travelers going?
- What obstacles of nature did they encounter along the trail?
- What did they take with them?
- Where does the trail begin and end?
- What do the symbols on the map stand for?
- What general direction does the trail go in?
- About how long is the trail?
- What types of events, adventures, disasters, or wildlife might have travelers encountered along the way?

Note: These questions and the ones that follow in the next paragraph are generic enough to use with many other trails and the like.

Next have students answer questions such as the following:

- Where on the map will they begin?
- What route will they travel?
- Will they travel as explorers, Native Americans, a family of settlers, 20th century tourists, or some other group?
- Along the way, will they pretend to be animals, landmarks (natural and man-made), and/or other features?
- What season are they traveling in and what kinds of weather will they deal with?
- What are some of the everyday activities they will show along the route?

Then show students how to map their journey on paper, translating the route they have chosen from the map, indicating obstacles, natural wonders, basic geography, and other features. Show them how to plot out the events, adventures, and disasters they plan to "experience."

Now have students create movement. Students can develop signature movements for animals and people, shapes for natural wonders, and locomotor movement patterns to show traveling. Finally, help students bring the map to life by guiding them as they combine the movements and phrases indicated on their version of the map to create a dance.

Sample Activity (5-8)

After researching the circulatory system, help students follow how the blood travels through the body. Have students make a diagram of the circulatory system as well as write a report on the subject.

Then direct students to create movements that represent veins, arteries, ventricles, aorta, red and white corpuscles, capillaries, oxygenated blood, blood traveling to and from lungs, and so on. Finally, have students arrange movement patterns to create a dance depicting the circulatory system.

Sample Activity (9-12)

Referring to *Gulliver's Travels,* have students draw a map of the journey and add details of Gulliver's adventures along the way. Then direct students to create a whole "ballet" or dance piece about his travels.

Assessment Form for Map-a-Dance

Outcome desired: Create a dance that depicts a journey taken along a mapped route.

Criteria	Dance Standards
Dance has movement at low, middle, and high levels and straight and curved pathways.	National Dance Content Standard 1 National Standard for Physical Education 2
Portfolio shows evidence of seven steps of building a dance.	National Dance Content Standard 2 National Standard for Physical Education 2
Students demonstrate good teamwork.	National Standard for Physical Education 7
Dance has a beginning, middle, and end.	National Dance Content Standard 2
Dance is set to music.	National Dance Content Standard 7 National Standards for Arts Education Music 8
Dance accurately depicts the route of a map.	New Standards: Applied Learning A3a
Dance shows evidence of an understanding of map skills.	New Standards: Applied Learning A3a
Researched facts are evident in dance.	New Standards: Applied Learning A3a

Portfolio Evidence/Work

- Video of created dance
- Evidence of research, e.g., sample maps and charts
- Evidence/documentation of seven steps of building a dance, e.g., Step 1: Write a paragraph about why you chose the map you did
- Completed self-, teacher, and peer evaluation forms

Rubric

3 = Above standard: The dance addresses all criteria and is executed at performance-quality level. Piece is revised based on teacher, peer, and self-evaluations. Portfolio work is completed.

2 = At standard: The dance addresses all criteria and is shared with the class. Portfolio work is completed.

1 = Below standard: The dance is missing some of the criteria but is shared with the class. Portfolio work is not complete or revised.

Score: _____   Name of evaluator: _____

(check one): Teacher _____   Peer _____   Self _____

Mask Dance

Purpose

In this activity, masks provide dance-making inspiration while teaching students how and why masks are used in different cultures.

Resources Needed

- Books about masks
- A collection of masks
- Mask-making materials
- Art teacher
- Books about fables
- Animal pictures
- Animal videos

General Procedure

Decide on a subject for your masks. Then have students research masks pertaining to the selected subject. They can bring in pictures or actual masks. When all the information is gathered, have the students design and construct the masks. Once mask construction is underway, direct the students, relying on the research and their imaginations, to develop movement phrases that depict the characters their masks portray (see figure 8.16). Another option is to allow students to use already-existing masks around which to create a dance, following the seven steps of building a dance.

Figure 8.16 Wearing a mask can make you feel very different.

Sample Activity (K-4)

Stage a Chinese New Year celebration. Help students research the celebration, the masks worn at the celebration, the parade, and who takes part. Provide the materials for them to copy, such as the masks of dragons, lions, snakes, devils, and gods from pictures or create some of their own, depicting other traditional characters.

   Next, guide each student to develop a signature movement for his or her mask character, developing dance patterns to enhance the natural movement of the character. Several students may also work together to make a giant dragon. (Simply add cloth to cover the people making up the body.) When all the masks and movements are set, you and your students are ready for a public celebration.

Sample Activity (5-8)

Have students read fables and make animal masks, depicting the characters in the fables. Then have them create dances to retell the fables.

Sample Activity (9-12)

Choose a theme, such as prejudice. Have students create two sets of solid-colored masks. Finally, challenge students to create a dance depicting conflict and resolution between the two groups.

Assessment Form for Mask Dance

Outcome desired: Construct a dance that shows how and why masks are used in different cultures.

Criteria	Dance Standards
Dance depicts the characteristics of the masks.	National Dance Content Standards 1, 2, & 4
Portfolio shows evidence of seven steps of building a dance.	National Standard for Physical Education 2 National Dance Content Standard 2
Researched facts are evident in dance.	New Standards: Applied Learning A3a
Dance has a clear beginning, middle, and end.	National Dance Content Standard 2
Students explain how and why masks are used in different cultures.	New Standards: Applied Learning A2a
Dance is set to music (optional).	National Dance Content Standard 7 National Standards for Arts Education: Music 8
Students make their own masks.	National Dance Content Standard 7 National Standards for Arts Education: Visual Arts 6
Student uses full body movement to depict character.	National Dance Content Standard 2 National Standard for Physical Education 1
Students demonstrate teamwork	National Standard for Physical Education 5 & 7

Portfolio Evidence/Work

- Masks
- Video of created dance
- Evidence of research, e.g., pictures of masks from various countries
- Evidence/documentation of seven steps of building a dance, e.g., Step 6: Picture of a mask of your own design and creation
- Completed self-, teacher, and peer evaluation forms

Rubric

3 = Above standard: The dance addresses all criteria and is executed at performance-quality level. Piece is revised based on teacher, peer, and self-evaluations. Portfolio work is completed.

2 = At standard: The dance addresses all criteria and is shared with the class. Portfolio work is completed.

1 = Below standard: The dance is missing some of the criteria but is shared with the class. Portfolio work is not complete or revised.

Score: _____   Name of evaluator: _____

(check one): Teacher _____   Peer _____   Self _____

Purpose

In this activity, student movement skills and movement vocabulary will increase through using task cards. Each card has two different movement skills or concepts printed on it for a total of 108 movement skills and concepts.

Resources Needed

- More Deal-a-Dance cards (see page 116)

General Procedure

The all-new More Deal-a-Dance task card set is divided into four categories: "More Creative Movement Suggestions," "More Sport and Game Movements," "More Elements That Change Movement," and "More Dance Techniques and Basic Movements." The information on both the front and back of these cards can be the source for all the movements you and your students need to build any of the dance construction models (and any other dances). They may also serve as the method by which you may build your students' dance vocabularies.

In the following sections, we explain the purpose and goal of each of the four card categories.

More Creative Movement Suggestions

The 32 cards in this section promote creativity among reluctant students. In general, as soon as these students are given some suggestions, they come up with all sorts of ideas and movements on their own. Keep in mind, however, that the first time you try this is the hardest. Simply use the cards as ice breakers that build confidence. The "Try This" sections will provide additional motivation and fun.

More Sport and Game Movements

Each of the 24 cards in this category describes a different sport or game movement for students to imitate. Each card also tells what dance move it approximates, explaining the common ground between the two fields. Even the nondancer will be at ease when exploring movement and turning it into dance with these cards. Indeed, even if a student cannot perform a sport skill perfectly, the posturing or gist of the movement can lead to dance-making as long as he or she follows safety guidelines.

More Elements That Change Movement

This category of 16 cards is another way to get reluctant students to move without their thinking they are "dancing." As is explained in part III, this system, with its descriptive definitions and vocabulary, is useful in observing, describing, and improving movement. Specifically, this set of cards takes you through the categories of weight, time, space, and flow as a way of producing movement.

More Dance Techniques and Basic Movements

What does the word *technique* mean as applied to dance? We offer several viewpoints as there is much confusion as to what the term means in dance. Ballet, tap, modern, jazz, lyrical, world dance, ballroom, to name a few, are all dance *disciplines*. Within each discipline's framework, dancers may follow different techniques. Used this way, the term refers to personal modifications in how and what the "masters" teach, a body of knowledge, and the skills that have been developed to support the discipline. For example, ballet has Vagonova, Cechetti, and Royal Academy of Dance as distinct techniques. Recent ballet masters have added and embellished on these. Modern dance has the Graham, Humphrey/Weidman, Hanya Holm, and Horton as basic techniques. The newer masters have added their influences. In the field of jazz and stage dancing (or musical comedy), we see Luigi, Bob Fosse, and Matt Maddox as pioneers of the techniques of jazz dance. Choreographers prior to those just mentioned came from the areas of ballet and modern dance. Some of these choreographers include Jerome Robbins, Agnes De Mille, and Marge and Gower Champion. Lastly, Hollywood and television brought their own techniques to the public . . . Busby Berkley, Bill "Bojangles" Robinson, Fred Astaire, Gene Kelly, the Nicholas Brothers, Gregory Hines, and now Savion Glover.

Another definition of the term *technique* within the field of dance involves an actual skill or movement itself. Specifically, exhibiting "good technique" equals demonstrating the proper way to do it, how to do it safely, and how to master it. We might say, "He has wonderful technique," meaning he can perform the skill masterfully.

Sometimes confused with the term *technique* are the terms *style* and *stylized*. Gene Kelly, for example, had a definite style—a way of moving—people still recognize. So did Fred Astaire. Both men could also stylize their movements to set time, place, and character. In *On the Town*, for example, Gene Kelly dances his interpretation of how he thought a sailor would move.

The 36 cards in this category each give you both a definition of the term covered and instructions as to how to execute the movement. In addition, each card gives you a derivation of the movement or step. Finally, to enhance creativity, a section listing several ways to vary the movement or step is called "Try This."

Ways to Use the Cards

First of all, we suggest copying the cards onto four different colors of stock, or thicker, paper. You and your students will be able to more easily identify the four categories of the cards if they are on different colors of paper. A sample card with its various parts labeled is shown in figure 8.17. As you can see, you may use the cards in a variety of ways. As a quick example, you or your students may select (choosing randomly or not) a few cards from each of several categories and combine them to create a movement pattern or dance. You may then help facilitate the process by setting the order students use the cards in (e.g., by category). Have students work together as a whole class, in small groups, or as individual students. If desired, add appropriate music. The following lists other activities you and your students can do using the More Deal-a-Dance cards:

More Sport and Game Movements

Playing Hopscotch

Description: Map out a course on the ground with chalk. It should include numbers 1 up to 10. Toss a stone or other heavy object onto one of the numbered blocks. Hop into individual boxes in numerical order until you get to that box, bend over and retrieve the object, then hop back to home base, being careful not to step on a line.

Try This

- Stretch for your object (stone), pretending it is two blocks away.
- Lose your balance, regain it, lose it again, and fall.
- Go through the whole course two times.
- Go through the course in reverse.
- Go through the course turned backward.
- Do the course with wrists (right to left) tied together.

Figure 8.17 A sample More Deal-a-Dance card.

- Teach two or three movement skills per lesson, working toward building a bigger dance and movement vocabulary.
- Explore the "Try This" sections on the cards.
- Combine several of the skills. Also try varying them.
- Divide students into groups of three to five and complete the following tasks.

1. Give each group a number of cards and have them arrange them in an order of their own design.
2. Have them lay the cards out on the floor in front of them and try their arrangement, changing it until they are satisfied.
3. Once they have set the order, direct them to link the movements from each card. Explain they can make transitions by adding other movement patterns or simply moving from one movement to the next.
4. Encourage them to clearly define the beginning and end of their sequence by freezing the starting position of the first movement and holding the ending position of the last movement.
5. Finally, have groups perform their dances for each other.

- Assign a specified number of counts (beats) to each movement or to the entire movement sequence for students to implement.
- To add music to this activity, teach the class to clap out the beat and then organize the musical selection to use when dance-making.
- Have the class do any developed sequence in reverse order.

Sample Activity (K-4)

Place the following three "More Dance Techniques and Basic Movements" cards on the floor: "Digging"—putting the heel of one foot on the ground while the toe points upward; "Twisting"—keeping the feet in a stationary position while rotating the body varying degrees; and "Brushing"—lifting the foot with knee bent, then thrusting the foot forward until the leg is straight, scraping the floor in the process. Add a "More Sport and Game Movements" card: "Hurdling." Show students how to put the four movements together to make a movement pattern, labeling the movements "one" through "four." To extend this activity, vary when you do the movements as individuals and then as a group. For example, one-third of the group "digs," one-third "twists," and one-third "brushes"—then they all "hurdle."

Sample Activity (5-8)

Divide the class into three groups. Give each group different "More Creative Movement Suggestions" cards. Have each group create a movement pattern using the first four cards they draw from the "More Creative Movement Suggestions" category.

Sample Activity (9-12)

Allow students to select several "More Creative Movement Suggestions" cards with the subcategory of "Everyday Movements." Have the students explore those activities integrating four different movements from the "More Dance Techniques and Basic Movements" cards as their base. They may run, skip, walk, and hop. If desired, you may have them add linking movements to make the phrase longer. When the movement patterns or dance piece have been refined, direct students to incorporate "More Elements That Change Movement" cards.

Assessment Form for More Deal-a-Dance

Outcome desired: Construct a dance using movement skills and vocabulary from the More Deal-a-Dance cards.

Criteria	Dance Standards
The dance includes skills and vocabulary from the cards.	National Dance Content Standard 1 National Standard for Physical Education 2
Portfolio shows evidence of seven steps of building a dance.	National Dance Content Standard 2 National Standard for Physical Education 2
Information from the cards is evident in dance.	New Standards: Applied Learning A3a
Dance has a clear beginning, middle, and end.	National Dance Content Standard 2
Students explain the process used in making the dance from the cards.	New Standards: Applied Learning A2a
Dance is set to music (optional).	National Dance Content Standard 7 National Standards for Arts Education: Music 8

Portfolio Evidence/Work

- Video of created dance
- Evidence of research, e.g., a list of cards chosen as the basis for choreography
- Evidence/documentation of seven steps of building a dance, e.g., Step 4: Written combinations of the order of the movements and suggested transition movements
- Completed self-, teacher, and peer evaluation forms

Rubric

3 = Above standard: The dance addresses all criteria and is executed at performance-quality level. Piece is revised based on teacher, peer, and self-evaluations. Portfolio work is completed.

2 = At standard: The dance addresses all criteria and is shared with the class. Portfolio work is completed.

1 = Below standard: The dance is missing some of the criteria but is shared with the class. Portfolio work is not complete or revised.

Score: _____   Name of evaluator: _____

(check one): Teacher _____   Peer _____   Self _____

Mythology Dance

Purpose

In this activity, students will learn more about myths and legends through analyzing mythological characters and their traits and translating the written word into movement.

Resources Needed

- Books retelling myths
- Pictures of mythological characters and creatures
- A classroom/language arts teacher

General Procedure

Have students read about or listen to several myths from a particular culture, as a class project or homework assignment. Show them artwork depicting one or more myths and its characters and creatures. Discuss with students mythology in general and the specific facts of the ones they read. In addition, discuss the types of creatures found in myths and research any present day myths. Then have students create a dance retelling a myth (see figure 8.18).

Figure 8.18   Mythical characters inspire innovative movement.

Sample Activity (K-4)

Read, or have students read, one or more of Aesop's Fables. Help students re-create these creatures by drawing them, designing and making costumes, or using makeup. Then help them create movement patterns or signatures to depict these creatures. Finally, have small groups create original stories, connecting the creatures.

Sample Activity (5-8)

Have students study the *Hobbit.* Guide them as they discuss and analyze the characters and creatures in this classic tale. Then have them create a dance or dances showing the nature of the characters and how they react to the others in the story. They can do this as individuals first, one character or creature at a time. Then they can link them by forming a small group, and these groups can then link until they can tell the story.

Sample Activity (9-12)

Work with the language arts teachers to have the students study the *Odyssey* or the *Iliad.* Proceed as for fifth to eighth graders. If desired, have students perfect their dances to performance level, depicting the whole myth in a live performance.

Assessment Form for Mythology Dance

Outcome desired: Construct a dance from myths and the characters and creatures in them.

Criteria	Dance Standards
The dance depicts the myths, characters, and creatures.	National Dance Content Standard 3
Portfolio shows evidence of seven steps of building a dance.	National Standard for Physical Education 2 National Dance Content Standard 2
Researched facts are evident in dance.	New Standards: Applied Learning A3a
Dance has a clear beginning, middle, and end.	National Dance Content Standard 2
Students verbally tell the story and then dance it.	New Standards: Applied Learning A2a
Dance is set to music (optional).	National Dance Content Standard 7 National Standards for Arts Education: Music 8

Portfolio Evidence/Work

- Video of created dance
- Evidence of research, e.g., highlights of a chosen myth
- Evidence/documentation of seven steps of building a dance, e.g., Step 6: Sketches or pictures of masks, costumes, or props to enhance dance
- Completed self-, teacher, and peer evaluation forms

Rubric

3 = Above standard: The dance addresses all criteria and is executed at performance-quality level. Piece is revised based on teacher, peer, and self-evaluations. Portfolio work is completed.

2 = At standard: The dance addresses all criteria and is shared with the class. Portfolio work is completed.

1 = Below standard: The dance is missing some of the criteria but is shared with the class. Portfolio work is not complete or revised.

Score: _____   Name of evaluator: _____

(check one): Teacher _____   Peer _____   Self _____

Rhythmatron Dance

Purpose

In this activity, students will become more aware of how percussive rhythms may impact movement choices. They experiment with this relationship and *syncopation*, which is a musical interruption of a regular, measured beat.

Resources Needed

- Small percussion instruments (e.g., triangles, lummi sticks, castanets)
- African drums
- Tapes or CDs of percussion music (e.g., Mickey Hart), African drum music, or Latin steel drums
- Videos such as *Stomp, Tap Dogs, Riverdance*

General Procedure

Discuss the definition of *beat*, that is, a steady, even, regular interval of sound and silence. For example, the "tick-tock" of a clock has a steady beat. Then discuss the definition of *rhythm*, that is, the periodic emphasis of, and in addition to, a beat. If you count "1, 2, 3, 4," that is the beat. If you add an "and" between any of the numbers, you have created a rhythm. For example, the meshing of gears of a motor and the swishing of windshield wipers can have definite rhythms. Next, discuss the definition of *timing*, meaning speed of the rhythm (faster or slower). For example, a steam locomotive has the same rhythm but may become progressively faster and then slower. Now discuss *syncopation*, or the musical interruption of a regular beat. For example, your heartbeat is syncopated: ba BAM, ba BAM, ba BAM. Now that students are familiar with these definitions, together, listen to music and watch videos, listening for and discussing which sounds are examples of a beat, which are examples of a rhythm, and which are examples of syncopation.

Sample Activity (K-4)

Have students sit on the floor. Start clapping evenly, counting to eight and repeating that eight. Show half the class how to keep the even beat and the other half how to clap on the "&" between the numbers: (1 & 2 & 3 & 4 & 5 & 6 & 7 & 8). Alternate which children clap when. Now have the children stand and put the beat in their feet or use their hands on different parts of their bodies.

Once students are comfortable with this beat as nonlocomotor movement, have them explore a locomotor movement to the same beat. (Remember, this has to be an even beat.) After some practice, guide the children to combine the nonlocomotor and locomotor movements into a movement phrase or a short dance. Finally, embellish the dance by letting the children use percussion instruments instead of, or along with, clapping (see figure 8.19).

Sample Activity (5-8)

Students at this level are able to develop intricate rhythm patterns. Start by telling students they will function as a band or orchestra with different students "playing" different rhythms that will blend into the basic beat. Divide the students into two groups: the *clappers* will create a rhythmic pattern, and the *steppers* will move to the clappers' pattern. After working out the beat with their hands and bodies as a nonlocomotor pattern, help them begin to explore and develop these rhythms to include locomotor movement.

1	&	2	&	3	&	4			
Step	Clap	Step	Clap	Step	Clap	Step			

5	&	a	6	&	a	7	&	an	8
Step	Clap	Clap	Step	Clap	Clap	Step	Clap	Clap	Step

When students' feet and bodies are synchronized, direct them to change floor patterns, switch who the steppers and who the clappers are, and change levels (at a low level, students may clap by hitting the floor). Next, assign small groups and have each group develop its own rhythm pattern. Finally, combine the groups' patterns to create a rhythm dance.

Sample Activity (9–12)

This activity helps high schoolers develop and perform a *Stomp*-like dance piece. Start by having students collect and bring in anything that will make percussive sounds. They don't have to be "loud" or traditional instruments; for example, a good broom makes an excellent swishing sound. Have students develop a steady beat and then a rhythmical pattern or patterns to that beat. Then direct them to take the beat and add locomotor and nonlocomotor movement phrases to the rhythms. Finally, have them link the sounds and movements together while arranging them in a logical, interesting format.

Figure 8.19 Percussive sounds can be made in many interesting ways and with many objects.

Assessment Form for Rhythmatron Dance

Outcome desired: Construct a dance using different rhythms and syncopation.

Criteria	Dance Standards
Dance uses different rhythms and syncopations.	National Dance Content Standards 1, 2, & 3 National Standard for Physical Education 2 National Standards for Arts Education: Music 8
Portfolio shows evidence of seven steps of building a dance.	National Dance Content Standard 2 National Standard for Physical Education 2
Dance has a clear beginning, middle, and end.	National Dance Content Standard 2
Students can explain the difference between *beat* and *rhythm*.	New Standards: Applied Learning A2a
Students set dance to rhythmical accompaniment.	National Dance Content Standard 7 National Standards for Arts Education: Music 8

Portfolio Evidence/Work

- Video of created dance
- Evidence of research, e.g., recordings of sample rhythms (in syncopation)
- Evidence/documentation of seven steps of building a dance, e.g., Step 6: Written chart of rhythms
- Completed self-, teacher, and peer evaluation forms

Rubric

3 = Above standard: The dance addresses all criteria and is executed at performance-quality level. Piece is revised based on teacher, peer, and self-evaluations. Portfolio work is completed.

2 = At standard: The dance addresses all criteria and is shared with the class. Portfolio work is completed.

1 = Below standard: The dance is missing some of the criteria but is shared with the class. Portfolio work is not complete or revised.

Score: _____ Name of evaluator: _____

(check one): Teacher _____ Peer _____ Self _____

Scavenger Hunt Dance

Purpose

In this activity, students will use items collected during a scavenger hunt as props or as inspiration for movement to create a dance, increasing student awareness of things around them, encouraging teamwork, enhancing problem-solving and research skills, and honing observation skills. And—oh, yes—it's fun!

Resources Needed

- Some "planted" items (optional)
- Permission from and a warning to your fellow faculty about this event

General Procedure

Create a list of items. Divide students into teams, and have them find these items and report where they found them. Then have them create signature movements or movement patterns to depict the objects. Next direct them to link these movements to create a dance. If they are able to have the object in hand, they may also build a movement pattern using the object as a prop (see figure 8.20).

Figure 8.20   Any prop can lead to building a dance.

Sample Activity (K-4)

Brainstorming articles in the school, together come up with a list such as the following: broom, trash basket, chalk, traffic cones, pencil, and paper. Send small groups off to find these objects. When they come back with the items, help them create a movement pattern or shape for each and then link the moves.

Sample Activity (5-8)

Have small groups each brainstorm their own list of several items to retrieve. Place each name of an item on a slip of paper, then place each slip into a hat or bag. Next have teams of students select 20 items that become their responsibility for finding as homework (we suggest assigning this task over a weekend). It is also helpful to have each team subdivide their list so that each member does one part. Warn teams not to divulge their lists to the other teams. Award teams one point for each item retrieved for a possible total of 20 points.

Finally, have each team create a story dance using the items as props. Give them up to 10 points for their story, based on an evaluation by a neutral panel. This panel can be made up of classroom teachers, parents, administrators, or peers. Give the team with the highest score out of 30 points a small prize.

Sample Activity (9-12)

Choose a topic, time period, or other theme on which to do a research scavenger hunt, such as the 15th century in Europe. Prepare a list of items, such as the food, games, dances, music, architecture, artwork, clothes, important events, religions, famous or infamous people, celebrations, facts about everyday life, occupations, education, and government. Let students form groups now to subdivide the work more efficiently. Let groups assign individuals to research each of these items, documenting evidence of research activities in the form of note cards, fact sheets printed from the Internet, and photocopies of information from reference books. Allow students to form groups, pool their research, and use their research as they follow the seven steps of building a dance to create a dance about Europe in the 15th century.

Assessment Form for Scavenger Hunt Dance

Outcome desired: Construct a dance using the props or information collected from the scavenger hunt.

Criteria	Dance Standards
Students use the props or information collected as inspiration for the dance.	National Dance Content Standards 1, 2, & 4 National Standard for Physical Education 2
Portfolio shows evidence of seven steps of building a dance.	National Dance Content Standard 2 National Standard for Physical Education 2
Researched facts are evident in dance.	New Standards: Applied Learning A3a
Dance has a clear beginning, middle, and end.	National Dance Content Standard 2
Students explain how they went from inspiration to movement (the dance).	New Standards: Applied Learning A2a
Dance is set to music (optional).	National Dance Content Standard 7 National Standards for Arts Education: Music 8
Students demonstrate teamwork.	National Standard for Physical Education 7

Portfolio Evidence/Work

- Video of created dance
- Evidence of research, e.g., total number of items from scavenger hunt list
- Evidence/documentation of seven steps of building a dance, e.g., Step 3: List three pieces of music and talk about how to change the selected movements
- Completed self-, teacher, and peer evaluation forms

Rubric

3 = Above standard: The dance addresses all criteria and is executed at performance-quality level. Piece is revised based on teacher, peer, and self-evaluations. Portfolio work is completed.

2 = At standard: The dance addresses all criteria and is shared with the class. Portfolio work is completed.

1 = Below standard: The dance is missing some of the criteria but is shared with the class. Portfolio work is not complete or revised.

Score: _____ Name of evaluator: _____

(check one): Teacher _____ Peer _____ Self _____

Sculpture and Shape Dance

Purpose

In this activity, students will observe three-dimensional objects, exploring them from different points of view. This activity also stresses the importance of revision and refining throughout the dance-making process.

Resources Needed

- Pictures of sculptures
- Trips to museums
- Books about sculptures and sculpting
- Art teacher

General Procedure

Take students to a gallery or park or provide photos from artwork books. In addition, help students observe everyday three-dimensional objects as well as sculptures from various points of view. As is age-appropriate, explain and discuss the meanings of *three-dimensional* versus *two-dimensional*. Then direct students to use these objects as inspiration for their dance-making. They can go from one image to another, shaping a beginning, a middle, and an end. Show them they can make sculptures come alive with movement and music (see figure 8.21)! In addition, help students recognize that, throughout the process, revision plays a key role—just as a sculptor reshapes a piece of clay.

Figure 8.21   You can be inspired by a piece of artwork that may have many shapes within it.

Sample Activity (K-4)

Show the entire class a variety of photographs or sculptures. Have them re-create what they see with their bodies. Choose an order for the re-created shapes so the dance has a beginning, a middle, and an end. Then link the poses with movement. Children can move as a whole class or in tandem.

Sample Activity (5-8)

Have students observe that it takes many pieces to create a whole image. A variation is for one student to act as the artist, "molding" the other students into a living work of art. You may divide the class into two groups so each may observe each other and make revisions. Encourage students to observe from all angles to see and mold from different points of view.

Sample Activity (9-12)

After taking students to observe sculptures at a gallery or park, choose or allow students to choose a theme from which to create a "still life," or "tableau." For example, scenes such as Mount Rushmore and the Iwo Jima Memorial can lead to a study of the history surrounding these. Then direct students to bring their tableaux to life through dance and movement. As an alternative, work with the art teacher to have students create their own abstract sculptures and then bring these to life. For all dances, if desired, encourage students to add simple costumes and props to revise and strengthen their "sculptures."

Assessment Form for Sculpture and Shape Dance

Outcome desired: Construct a dance based on observing a three-dimensional object from different points of view (viewing positions).

Criteria	Dance Standards
Dance depicts the visual artwork from different viewing positions.	National Dance Content Standards 2 & 3 National Standard for Physical Education 2 National Standards for Arts Education: Visual Arts 6
Portfolio shows evidence of seven steps of building a dance.	National Dance Content Standard 2 National Standard for Physical Education 2
Researched facts are evident in dance.	New Standards: Applied Learning A3a
Dance has a clear beginning, middle, and end.	National Dance Content Standard 2
Students can explain how the audience's viewpoint changes the understanding of the dance.	New Standards: Applied Learning A2a
Dance is set to music (optional).	National Dance Content Standard 7 National Standards for Arts Education: Music 8

Portfolio Evidence/Work

- Video of created dance
- Evidence of research, e.g., pictures of sculptures
- Evidence/documentation of seven steps of building a dance, e.g., Step 5: Video of the created movement phrase three times to judge whether it is done the same way
- Completed self-, teacher, and peer evaluation forms

Rubric

3 = Above standard: The dance addresses all criteria and is executed at performance-quality level. Piece is revised based on teacher, peer, and self-evaluations. Portfolio work is completed.

2 = At standard: The dance addresses all criteria and is shared with the class. Portfolio work is completed.

1 = Below standard: The dance is missing some of the criteria but is shared with the class. Portfolio work is not complete or revised.

Score: _____ Name of evaluator: _____

_____ (check one): Teacher _____ Peer _____ Self _____

Seesaw Dance

Purpose

In this activity, students will explore how the body functions as an instrument of communication and performance through experiencing how muscles work to make the body move in dance.

Resources Needed

- Rubber bands, hair "scrunchies," or bungee cords as models
- Pictures and/or models of muscles and joints
- Eyewitness video: *Skeleton*
- Magic School Bus video: *Magic School Bus Flexes Its Muscles*
- Towel

General Procedure

After doing research and hearing you describe and demonstrate the pulling action of muscles and the lengthening and shortening relationships between muscle groups, give students a chance to explore the movements made possible by these actions and relationships. From these explorations, let students build a dance (see figure 8.22).

Figure 8.22   For every action there is a reaction.

Sample Activity (K-4)

After demonstrating how a muscle pulls on a bone to create movement, help students safely explore how much force it takes to pull different light-to-heavy props. Then have students find partners with whom to explore the relationship between muscle groups (in technical terms, *antagonist* versus *protagonist*) through seesawing (students carefully pulling on each other, seesaw fashion). Next, have one partner carefully try to pull the other student forward in space without resistance, then with medium resistance (explaining how much resistance in age-appropriate terms). Then have students take turns pulling each other forward in space until they are across the dance space. You may also improvise and explore other partnered movements to create a movement vocabulary, which you may then organize into a seesaw muscle dance.

Sample Activity (5-8)

First, you will find that you may successfully use the K-4 activities with students in these grades. Then demonstrate and discuss isometric and isotonic muscle actions. As you discuss these concepts, emphasize the amount of resistance one muscle group gives to another: *Isometric* muscle actions show no movement because the amount of resistance of one muscle group balances that of the other muscle group. *Isotonic* muscle actions show movement because the amount of resistance of one muscle group is less than that of the other muscle group. A tug of war between partners or groups demonstrates these concepts well. Students may then explore pulling actions with varying amounts of resistance, using different shapes and connections other than hand to hand. You may then have students organize their explorations into an isotonic-isometric seesaw dance.

Sample Activity (9-12)

First explore the K-8 concepts with students. Then guide students to further explore the types of contractions that are possible in muscles: *concentric* (shortening) and *eccentric* (lengthening). Still using the seesaw idea, direct partners to provide resistance for each other through one partner's pulling into a small, tight shape or by slowly lengthening body shape and allowing the partner to pull him or her.

You may also relate the idea of *protagonistic* (group helps the movement) and *antagonistic* (group opposes the movement) muscle groups to literature, relationships, or social movements. Improvisation on this idea will produce movements students can combine or contrast, using concentric and eccentric movements. Finally, have students organize these movement phrases, set them to music, and perform a protagonist-antagonist dance.

Assessment Form for Seesaw Dance

Outcome desired: Construct a dance that shows how muscles work to move the body.

Criteria	Dance Standards
Dance shows how muscles work to move the body.	National Dance Content Standards 1, 2, 4, 6, & 7 National Science Education Standard 6 National Standards for Physical Education 1 & 2
Portfolio shows evidence of seven steps of building a dance.	National Dance Content Standard 2 National Standard for Physical Education 2
Researched facts are evident in dance.	New Standards: Applied Learning A3a
Dance has a clear beginning, middle, and end.	National Dance Content Standard 2
Students explain the relationships among muscle groups.	New Standards: Applied Learning A2a
Dance is set to music (optional).	National Dance Content Standard 7 National Standards for Arts Education: Music 8
Students demonstrate teamwork.	National Standards for Physical Education 5 & 7

Portfolio Evidence/Work

- Video of created dance
- Evidence of research, e.g., muscle charts
- Evidence/documentation of seven steps of building a dance, e.g., Step 4: Arrange different muscle sequences together and videotape them
- Completed self-, teacher, and peer evaluation forms

Rubric

3 = Above standard: The dance addresses all criteria and is executed at performance-quality level. Piece is revised based on teacher, peer, and self-evaluations. Portfolio work is completed.

2 = At standard: The dance addresses all criteria and is shared with the class. Portfolio work is completed.

1 = Below standard: The dance is missing some of the criteria but is shared with the class. Portfolio work is not complete or revised.

Score: _____   Name of evaluator: _____

(check one): Teacher _____   Peer _____   Self _____

Social Studies Dance

Purpose

In this activity, students will research, discuss, and study major social studies content for their grade level, then create dances to depict the content.

Resources Needed

- Newspaper and magazine articles on social issues
- Dictionaries
- Videos pertaining to the area of study
- Reference books pertaining to the area of study

General Procedure

After researching and defining a topic (e.g., cause and effect, prejudice, government, transportation, community, civics, industry), students create dances to depict the topic. The instructor along with students could look up the definitions in the dictionary.

Sample Activity (K-4)

Encourage students to work with the terms *community, transportation,* and *industry*. To build a dance, have them create people in their community, how they get around, and what work they do. Then have them link the concepts together to help them see how the three areas impact each other.

Sample Activity (5-8)

Encourage students to define the terms *prejudice* and *tolerance*. After introducing the terms, have them research the terms and the relationship between the two. Then guide them to deal with their feelings about these terms through the seven steps of building a dance and through the finished movement phrases. This will allow them to share their feelings in a nonthreatening atmosphere.

Figure 8.23   A peacemaker can soothe an angry person.

Sample Activity (9-12)

Have students define and explore *cause* and *effect* as this relationship pertains to social studies. Using their research for inspiration, direct each student to individually go through the seven steps of building a dance to create a formal or informal dance piece based on some aspect of the topic (see figure 8.23).

Assessment Form for Social Studies Dance

Outcome desired: Construct a dance based on a social studies topic.

Criteria	Dance Standards
Dance depicts the social studies topic.	National Dance Content Standards 2, 5, & 7 National Standard for Physical Education 2
Portfolio shows evidence of seven steps of building a dance.	National Dance Content Standard 2 National Standard for Physical Education 2
Researched facts are evident in dance.	New Standards: Applied Learning A3a
Dance has a clear beginning, middle, and end.	National Dance Content Standard 2
Students create a written report on the chosen social studies topic.	New Standards: English Language Arts E2d National Geography Standards, National Standards for U.S. History, or National Standards for History (depends on topic)
Dance is set to music (optional).	National Dance Content Standard 7 National Standards for Arts Education: Music 8
Students demonstrate teamwork.	National Standards for Physical Education 5 & 7

Portfolio Evidence/Work

- Video of created dance
- Evidence of research, e.g., short narrative of chosen social studies topic
- Evidence/documentation of seven steps of building a dance, e.g., Step 2: From pictures, create movement to portray the picture, and videotape the results
- Completed self-, teacher, and peer evaluation forms

Rubric

3 = Above standard: The dance addresses all criteria and is executed at performance-quality level. Piece is revised based on teacher, peer, and self-evaluations. Portfolio work is completed.

2 = At standard: The dance addresses all criteria and is shared with the class. Portfolio work is completed.

1 = Below standard: The dance is missing some of the criteria but is shared with the class. Portfolio work is not complete or revised.

Score: _____ Name of evaluator: _____

(check one): Teacher _____ Peer _____ Self _____

Appendix

Dance Construction Model Finder

Name of Dance Construction Model	NDCS	NSPE	Page number
Blueprint Dance	1, 2, 3, 7	1, 2	43
Carnivale	2, 3, 5, 7	2, 6	46
Communication Dance	2, 3, 7	2	48
Concepts and Basic Skills Dance	2, 3, 7	2	51
Countries Dance	1, 2, 3, 4, 5, 7	2, 6, 7	54
Create-a-Line Dance	1, 2, 7	2, 7	57
Dance-a-Quote	2, 3, 7	2, 7	60
Dance-a-Warm-Up	1, 2, 3, 6, 7	2, 4	63
Dance Is in the Bag	1, 2, 3, 4, 7	1, 2, 7	66
Dance Through History	2, 3, 5, 7	2	69
Dance Through Time	2, 3, 5, 7	2, 6, 7	72
Dancing at the Joint	1, 2, 4, 6, 7	1, 2, 5, 7	75
Field Trip Dance	2, 3, 7	2	78
Have a Healthy Heart Dance	1, 2, 6, 7	1, 2, 4	81
Map-a-Dance	1, 2, 7	2, 7	84
Mask Dance	1, 2, 4, 7	2, 5, 7	88
More Deal-a-Dance	1, 2, 7	2	91
Mythology Dance	2, 3, 7	2	96
Rhythmatron Dance	1, 2, 3, 7	2	99
Scavenger Hunt Dance	1, 2, 4, 7	2, 7	103
Sculpture and Shape Dance	2, 3, 7	2	106
Seesaw Dance	1, 2, 4, 6, 7	1, 2, 5, 7	109
Social Studies Dance	2, 5, 7	2, 5, 7	112

NDCS = National Dance Content Standards; NSPE = National Standards for Physical Education.

MORE Creative Movement Suggestions

Climbing

Try This

- Explore ways you might climb.
- Explore things that climb.
- Pretend you are a monkey climbing up a pole.
- Pretend you are ivy climbing up a tree.
- Pretend you are climbing a steep mountain.
- Pretend you are climbing on a jungle gym.
- Pretend you are climbing a rope.

From *Building More Dances* by Susan McGreevy-Nichols, Helene Scheff, and Marty Sprague, 2001, Champaign, IL: Human Kinetics.

MORE Creative Movement Suggestions

Going Over

Try This

- Explore ways you can get over something.
- Pretend something is going over you.
- Pretend you are reaching over something breakable.
- Pretend you are going over something very high.
- Pretend you are going over something very low.
- Pretend you are going over something very wide.
- Pretend you are going over something very narrow.

From *Building More Dances* by Susan McGreevy-Nichols, Helene Scheff, and Marty Sprague, 2001, Champaign, IL: Human Kinetics.

MORE
Creative Movement Suggestions

Hiding

Try This

- Pretend there is a high wall in front of you.
- Pretend someone or something is chasing you.
- Pretend you are trying to hide a small item.
- Pretend you are trying to hide a large item.
- Pretend you are being hidden by a soft, flexible item.
- In a group, create a "hide and find" sequence.

From *Building More Dances* by Susan McGreevy-Nichols, Helene Scheff, and Marty Sprague, 2001, Champaign, IL: Human Kinetics.

MORE
Creative Movement Suggestions

Trembling

Try This

- Explore times when you might tremble.
- Pretend you are something that might tremble.
- Explore having only one small part of your body tremble.
- Explore the feeling when that small part starts to engage (involve) the nearest parts.
- Pretend you are afraid.
- With a group, pretend you are rocks right before an avalanche.
- Pretend you are so excited you can't stand it.

From *Building More Dances* by Susan McGreevy-Nichols, Helene Scheff, and Marty Sprague, 2001, Champaign, IL: Human Kinetics.

Making Circles

Try This

- Make a circle with a finger.
- Make a circle with a leg.
- Make a circle with your head.
- Make a circle with an arm.
- Make a circle with your whole body.
- Link all your circles into one continuous movement.

From *Building More Dances* by Susan McGreevy-Nichols, Helene Scheff, and Marty Sprague, 2001, Champaign, IL: Human Kinetics.

Watching

Try This

- Pretend you are on the lookout for something in the distance.
- Pretend you are on the lookout for something nearby.
- Pretend you are following birds in flight.
- Pretend you are following ants.
- Pretend you are on the lookout for incoming planes.
- Pretend you are watching the funnel cloud of a tornado.

From *Building More Dances* by Susan McGreevy-Nichols, Helene Scheff, and Marty Sprague, 2001, Champaign, IL: Human Kinetics.

MORE Creative Movement Suggestions

Point

Try This

- Stare at something, showing it is coming closer and then moving farther away.
- Use your finger to show where something is.
- Make that object move.
- Get your whole body to show a direction.
- Make your arms show direction.
- Make your legs show direction.

From *Building More Dances* by Susan McGreevy-Nichols, Helene Scheff, and Marty Sprague, 2001, Champaign, IL: Human Kinetics.

MORE Creative Movement Suggestions

Attaching

Try This

- Put something together with pretend crazy glue.
- Put something together with pretend Velcro.
- Discover something stuck to your buns.
- With your foot, discover gum on the floor.
- Pretend your hands are stuck together.
- Pretend your feet and hands are stuck together.

From *Building More Dances* by Susan McGreevy-Nichols, Helene Scheff, and Marty Sprague, 2001, Champaign, IL: Human Kinetics.

Seeking

Try This

- Look for a lost object and find it.
- Search beach sand for seashells.
- Search the rosebuds for Japanese beetles and capture them.
- Look for a friend in a crowd.
- Search for socks your size on a table in a bargain store.
- Look for a particular book on library shelves.

From *Building More Dances* by Susan McGreevy-Nichols, Helene Scheff, and Marty Sprague, 2001, Champaign, IL: Human Kinetics.

Inspecting

Try This

- Carefully pretend to look over something with many parts.
- Pretend you are a detective looking for clues.
- Pretend you are a quality-control official.
- Examine an object and get rid of extra parts.
- Examine something from the refrigerator that has been there for a long time.
- In a group, create an assembly line of items to be inspected.

From *Building More Dances* by Susan McGreevy-Nichols, Helene Scheff, and Marty Sprague, 2001, Champaign, IL: Human Kinetics.

Being Bored

Try This

- Explore when you might be bored.
- Explore how to be bored without showing it.
- Make floor patterns with your feet while looking bored.
- Explore what makes you know when others are bored.
- Go from being bored to being very interested.
- In a group, create a "sculpture" that expresses various degrees, or levels, of boredom.

From *Building More Dances* by Susan McGreevy-Nichols, Helene Scheff, and Marty Sprague, 2001, Champaign, IL: Human Kinetics.

Avoiding

Try This

- Go through a newly painted doorway without getting wet.
- Go through a crowd and keep missing a particular person.
- Run through the rain, trying not to get wet.
- Pretend you are playing dodgeball.
- Pretend you are dodging an oncoming bicycle.
- Explore things you might want to avoid.

From *Building More Dances* by Susan McGreevy-Nichols, Helene Scheff, and Marty Sprague, 2001, Champaign, IL: Human Kinetics.

MORE Creative Movement Suggestions

Being Lazy

Try This

- Pretend it is a summer afternoon, and you are in a hammock under a tree.
- Pretend you have a large stack of books to move up the stairs with minimum effort.
- Pretend the fence needs painting, and you just don't want to do it.
- Rise up from the floor in slow motion.
- Pretend you are a lazy dog eating out of your bowl.
- The alarm goes off, and you do not want to get out of bed.

From *Building More Dances* by Susan McGreevy-Nichols, Helene Scheff, and Marty Sprague, 2001, Champaign, IL: Human Kinetics.

MORE Creative Movement Suggestions

Following

Try This

- Go down a specific path.
- In a group, play follow-the-leader, taking a linear path and taking turns being the leader.
- You do a movement phrase and others copy it.
- Do short movement patterns in a sequence.
- In a group, create a wave pattern.
- In a group, create a movement in unison, depicting robots.

From *Building More Dances* by Susan McGreevy-Nichols, Helene Scheff, and Marty Sprague, 2001, Champaign, IL: Human Kinetics.

Hanging

Try This

- Pretend you are a monkey in a tree.
- Pretend you are on a trapeze.
- Pretend you are a piece of clothing drying outdoors on a line.
- Pretend you are an article of clothing being hung.
- Hang tree ornaments.
- Pretend you are hang gliding.

From *Building More Dances* by Susan McGreevy-Nichols, Helene Scheff, and Marty Sprague, 2001, Champaign, IL: Human Kinetics.

Feeling Nervous

Try This

- Pretend you are meeting a new teacher.
- Pretend you just snitched the last cookie.
- Pretend you are playing soccer and have a corner kick.
- Pretend your team is down by one and you are shooting a free throw.
- Pretend you are in a huge performance and have not mastered the skill you must perform.
- Pretend you are baby-sitting for the first time.
- Pretend you are home alone for the first time.

From *Building More Dances* by Susan McGreevy-Nichols, Helene Scheff, and Marty Sprague, 2001, Champaign, IL: Human Kinetics.

MORE

Creative Movement Suggestions

Everyday Movements

Washing Windows

Try This

- Use your right arm.
- Use your left arm.
- Keep the sun out of your eyes.
- Find a smudge.
- Change level.
- Change speed.

From *Building More Dances* by Susan McGreevy-Nichols, Helene Scheff, and Marty Sprague, 2001, Champaign, IL: Human Kinetics.

MORE

Creative Movement Suggestions

Everyday Movements

Hanging Clothes

Try This

- Hang something heavy.
- Hang something while the wind is blowing.
- Hang something tiny.
- Pull a tangled mess out of the laundry basket.
- Try to hang something beyond your reach.

From *Building More Dances* by Susan McGreevy-Nichols, Helene Scheff, and Marty Sprague, 2001, Champaign, IL: Human Kinetics.

Directing an Airplane to the Gate

Try This

- Change direction.
- Change speed.
- Stop the plane "on a dime."
- Give the all-clear.
- Repeat the actions in a definite pattern.
- Develop a sequence for doing the job.

From *Building More Dances* by Susan McGreevy-Nichols, Helene Scheff, and Marty Sprague, 2001, Champaign, IL: Human Kinetics.

Directing Traffic

Try This

- Wave cars on.
- Stop the traffic flow.
- Hold traffic from one direction while moving others around.
- Do the movement in slow motion.
- Do the movement as if you were a robot.

From *Building More Dances* by Susan McGreevy-Nichols, Helene Scheff, and Marty Sprague, 2001, Champaign, IL: Human Kinetics.

MORE Creative Movement Suggestions

Everyday Movements

Sleeping

Try This

- Try to get comfortable.
- Pretend there is too much light.
- Wake up slowly.
- Pretend you are having a bad dream.
- Wake up to a loud alarm.
- Change position five times.

From *Building More Dances* by Susan McGreevy-Nichols, Helene Scheff, and Marty Sprague, 2001, Champaign, IL: Human Kinetics.

MORE Creative Movement Suggestions

Everyday Movements

Digging

Try This

- Pretend you are digging in hard dirt.
- Pretend you are digging a splinter out of your finger.
- Pretend you are digging while time is running out.
- Pretend you are looking for a lost treasure that is fragile.
- Pretend you are digging your heels into the ground so as not to lose your balance.
- Pretend you are digging up a delicate plant to transplant it.

From *Building More Dances* by Susan McGreevy-Nichols, Helene Scheff, and Marty Sprague, 2001, Champaign, IL: Human Kinetics.

MORE
Creative Movement Suggestions

Everyday Movements

Using an Umbrella

Try This

- Explore what happens to an umbrella in the wind.
- Pretend to open an umbrella that is stubborn (hard to open).
- Pretend you are singing in the rain.
- Use the umbrella as if you are on a tightrope.
- Use the umbrella as a shield against a sword.

From *Building More Dances* by Susan McGreevy-Nichols, Helene Scheff, and Marty Sprague, 2001, Champaign, IL: Human Kinetics.

MORE
Creative Movement Suggestions

Everyday Movements

Sweeping and Mopping

Try This

- Pretend you are using a huge broom.
- Pretend you are using an old broom with bad bristles.
- Mop yourself into a corner.
- Sweep to the right.
- Sweep to the left.
- Sweep it under the rug.

From *Building More Dances* by Susan McGreevy-Nichols, Helene Scheff, and Marty Sprague, 2001, Champaign, IL: Human Kinetics.

MORE
Creative Movement Suggestions

Everyday Movements

Waiting in Line

Try This

- See how long the line is.
- The person behind you is getting too close.
- Get bored.
- Get annoyed.
- Lose your place.

From *Building More Dances* by Susan McGreevy-Nichols, Helene Scheff, and Marty Sprague, 2001, Champaign, IL: Human Kinetics.

MORE
Creative Movement Suggestions

Everyday Movements

Using a Towel

Try This

- Dry the dishes.
- Dry your body.
- Wipe down a wall.
- Bat at your little sister.
- Use it as a toreador cape.

From *Building More Dances* by Susan McGreevy-Nichols, Helene Scheff, and Marty Sprague, 2001, Champaign, IL: Human Kinetics.

MORE
Creative Movement Suggestions

Everyday Movements

Surfacing

Try This

- Come up out of water.
- Come up from being buried in dirt or sand.
- Pretend you are a dolphin coming up for air and then submerging.
- Pretend you are a submarine.
- Come to the top of a pit filled with pieces of foam rubber.

From *Building More Dances* by Susan McGreevy-Nichols, Helene Scheff, and Marty Sprague, 2001, Champaign, IL: Human Kinetics.

MORE
Creative Movement Suggestions

Everyday Movements

Visiting the Ocean

Try This

- Run into icy water.
- Jump each wave.
- Outrun a wave.
- Pretend seaweed circles your legs.
- Pretend to swallow saltwater.

From *Building More Dances* by Susan McGreevy-Nichols, Helene Scheff, and Marty Sprague, 2001, Champaign, IL: Human Kinetics.

MORE Creative Movement Suggestions

Everyday Movements

Mowing and Raking

Try This

- Pretend to use a huge power riding lawn mower.
- Pretend to use an old push lawn mower.
- Rake the leaves in the wind.
- Jump into piles of leaves.
- Mow around trees and shrubs.
- Rake leaves into a huge pile and have wind blow them away.

From *Building More Dances* by Susan McGreevy-Nichols, Helene Scheff, and Marty Sprague, 2001, Champaign, IL: Human Kinetics.

MORE Creative Movement Suggestions

Everyday Movements

Walking

Try This

- Walk through tall grass.
- Walk on eggs.
- Walk on hot coals.
- Walk on ice.
- Walk in heavy snow.
- Walk against the wind.
- Walk uphill.

From *Building More Dances* by Susan McGreevy-Nichols, Helene Scheff, and Marty Sprague, 2001, Champaign, IL: Human Kinetics.

MORE Creative Movement Suggestions

Everyday Movements

Changing a Tire

Try This

- Pretend to change a tire while parked on a hill.
- Pretend to change a tire in the rain.
- Pretend the tire won't come loose.
- Pretend to change a tire during the Indy 500.
- Work in cooperation with a partner to change a tire.

From *Building More Dances* by Susan McGreevy-Nichols, Helene Scheff, and Marty Sprague, 2001, Champaign, IL: Human Kinetics.

MORE Creative Movement Suggestions

Everyday Movements

Picking Up

Try This

- Pick up a feather.
- Pick up a heavy rock.
- Pick up an uneven stack of books.
- Pick up a penny.
- Pick up a pile of clothes from the dryer.
- Pick up a box you thought was heavy but turns out to be light.
- Pick up a box you thought was light but turns out to be heavy.

From *Building More Dances* by Susan McGreevy-Nichols, Helene Scheff, and Marty Sprague, 2001, Champaign, IL: Human Kinetics.

MORE
Sport and Game Movements

Volleyball

Spiking

Description: Jump up to hit a ball you have set (tossed) above your head. Strike the ball downward.

Try This

- Hop while spiking.
- Run three steps before spiking.
- Gallop into the spike.
- Jump with a half turn while spiking the ball.
- Jump with a full turn while spiking the ball.

From *Building More Dances* by Susan McGreevy-Nichols, Helene Scheff, and Marty Sprague, 2001, Champaign, IL: Human Kinetics.

MORE
Sport and Game Movements

Track and Field Events

Hurdling

Description: This is leaping over an object, leading with one leg and carrying the other high behind.

Try This

- Take two steps between leaps.
- Lean forward while leaping.
- Keep arms out while leaping.
- Change direction.
- Change height.
- Do several leaps, running between and traveling in a circle.
- Create a short dance, using movements from three of the other ideas.

From *Building More Dances* by Susan McGreevy-Nichols, Helene Scheff, and Marty Sprague, 2001, Champaign, IL: Human Kinetics.

Playing Frisbee

Description: A Frisbee is a small, round plastic disk you toss and catch.

Try This

- Throw it from behind your back.
- Catch it behind your back.
- Throw it too short.
- Throw it too long.
- Throw it too low.
- Throw it too high.
- Turn and throw in one continuous movement.

From *Building More Dances* by Susan McGreevy-Nichols, Helene Scheff, and Marty Sprague, 2001, Champaign, IL: Human Kinetics.

Playing Hopscotch

Description: Map out a course on the ground with chalk. It should include numbers 1 up to 10. Toss a stone or other heavy object onto one of the numbered blocks. Hop into individual boxes in numerical order until you get to that box, bend over and retrieve the object, then hop back to home base, being careful not to step on a line.

Try This

- Stretch for your object (stone), pretending it is two blocks away.
- Lose your balance, regain it, lose it again, and fall.
- Go through the whole course two times.
- Go through the course in reverse.
- Go through the course turned backward.
- Do the course with wrists (right to left) tied together.

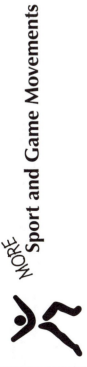

From *Building More Dances* by Susan McGreevy-Nichols, Helene Scheff, and Marty Sprague, 2001, Champaign, IL: Human Kinetics.

Serving Underhand

Description: Hold the ball with one hand and hit it over the net by swinging the other hand underhand.

Try This

- Pretend the volleyball is a puff of cotton.
- Pretend the volleyball is as heavy as a medicine ball.
- Show excitement after you serve because you won the point.
- Pretend the ball is stuck to your hand, and you can't get rid of it.
- Wind up and hit the ball.

From *Building More Dances* by Susan McGreevy-Nichols, Helene Scheff, and Marty Sprague, 2001, Champaign, IL: Human Kinetics.

Jumping Rope

Description: You can jump rope alone by holding one end of a rope in each hand or with two people each holding an end of the rope and a third person jumping as the other two turn the rope.

Try This

- Play double Dutch, making two ropes go in the opposite directions.
- Touch the ground in between jumps.
- Make a full turn while jumping.
- Do peppers, jumping fast with no little jump in between.
- Jumping alone, cross your hands with the rope.
- Do a hop-and-jump combination.
- Close your eyes and jump to the sound and rhythm of the rope.

From *Building More Dances* by Susan McGreevy-Nichols, Helene Scheff, and Marty Sprague, 2001, Champaign, IL: Human Kinetics.

Fishing

Try This

- Cast a line.
- Drop a line.
- Hook a fly and cast.
- Hook a heavy fish and reel in.
- Hook a little fish and reel in.
- Hook a shark.

From *Building More Dances* by Susan McGreevy-Nichols, Helene Scheff, and Marty Sprague, 2001, Champaign, IL: Human Kinetics.

Serving Overhand

Description: Toss the ball up in the air with one hand and strike it downward with the other.

Try This

- Jump while making the serve.
- Do the serve as a full-jump turn.
- Miss the ball.
- In a group, perform a sequence of serves.
- Hit the ball, then lose your balance.

From *Building More Dances* by Susan McGreevy-Nichols, Helene Scheff, and Marty Sprague, 2001, Champaign, IL: Human Kinetics.

Playing Tug-of-War

Try This

- Have more people on one side than the other.
- Pretend the ground below your feet is muddy.
- Pretend the ground below your feet is icy.
- Have someone on your side get distracted.
- Have everyone on one side let go.

From *Building More Dances* by Susan McGreevy-Nichols, Helene Scheff, and Marty Sprague, 2001, Champaign, IL: Human Kinetics.

Windsurfing

Try This

- Change sides (tack).
- Get blown over.
- Get caught in a storm.
- Change direction.
- Spot another boat heading in your direction.

From *Building More Dances* by Susan McGreevy-Nichols, Helene Scheff, and Marty Sprague, 2001, Champaign, IL: Human Kinetics.

MORE
Sport and Game Movements
Playground Activities

Seesawing

Try This

- Pretend to put several people on each end.
- See if you can balance the board, making it flat.
- Pretend to sit backward on the seesaw.
- Pretend a huge dog jumps on one end.
- Pretend the seesaw breaks in the middle as you get on.

From *Building More Dances* by Susan McGreevy-Nichols, Helene Scheff, and Marty Sprague, 2001, Champaign, IL: Human Kinetics.

MORE
Sport and Game Movements
Playground Activities

Sliding

Try This

- Walk up the slide.
- Slide down on your tummy.
- Slide down on your side.
- Slide down with your arms wrapped around your waist.
- Slide down in slow motion.

From *Building More Dances* by Susan McGreevy-Nichols, Helene Scheff, and Marty Sprague, 2001, Champaign, IL: Human Kinetics.

MORE **Sport and Game Movements**

Swimming

Swimming Butterfly

Try This

- Use only your right arm.
- Use only your left arm.
- Use this stroke going through mud.
- Use this stroke going through air.
- Use this stroke to go backward.

From *Building More Dances* by Susan McGreevy-Nichols, Helene Scheff, and Marty Sprague, 2001, Champaign, IL: Human Kinetics.

MORE **Sport and Game Movements**

Playground Activities

Climbing on a Jungle Gym

Try This

- Climb in a crawling position.
- Hang from the top by your knees.
- Climb, using only your right foot and left arm.
- Climb, using only your left foot and right arm.
- Climb in a specific pattern and then reverse the pattern coming down.

From *Building More Dances* by Susan McGreevy-Nichols, Helene Scheff, and Marty Sprague, 2001, Champaign, IL: Human Kinetics.

Bowling

Try This

- Bowl a strike.
- Bowl a gutter ball.
- Make the last pin drop.
- Use both hands to send the ball.
- Lob the ball and follow the movement with your head (focusing and following through).
- Have a finger get stuck in the ball.
- Invent a "new" approach.

From *Building More Dances* by Susan McGreevy-Nichols, Helene Scheff, and Marty Sprague, 2001, Champaign, IL: Human Kinetics.

Trotting

Description: This involves an even gait that is almost prance-like. In other words, each trot is a prance. This means exchanging your weight from one foot to the other and lifting the "free" foot with your knee bent in front of you.

Try This

- Make a pattern with four trots in each sequence.
- Trot backward.
- Trot with a partner.
- Trot in a circular pattern.
- Trot, pausing between each step.
- Show you are sitting on the horse while it is trotting.

From *Building More Dances* by Susan McGreevy-Nichols, Helene Scheff, and Marty Sprague, 2001, Champaign, IL: Human Kinetics.

MORE
Sport and Game Movements

Swimming

Swimming Backstroke

Description: Lying on your back, you rotate your arms alternately from front to back.

Try This

- Change level.
- Change direction.
- Change speed.
- Let your upper body follow your arms, moving across the activity area.
- Walk in any direction while doing the backstroke.
- Jump with each arm rotation.

From *Building More Dances* by Susan McGreevy-Nichols, Helene Scheff, and Marty Sprague, 2001, Champaign, IL: Human Kinetics.

MORE
Sport and Game Movements

Archery

Shooting an Arrow

Try This

- Pretend the bow is very tight.
- Show the arrow drops to the ground.
- Draw the bow in slow motion.
- Show you have hit your target.
- Shoot high.

From *Building More Dances* by Susan McGreevy-Nichols, Helene Scheff, and Marty Sprague, 2001, Champaign, IL: Human Kinetics.

MORE
Sport and Game Movements

Horseback Riding

Rowing a Boat

Try This

- Use only your right arm.
- Use only your left arm.
- Go forward.
- Go backward.
- Go really fast.

From *Building More Dances* by Susan McGreevy-Nichols, Helene Scheff, and Marty Sprague, 2001, Champaign, IL: Human Kinetics.

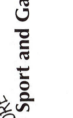

MORE
Sport and Game Movements

Horseback Riding

Cantering

Description: This involves uneven gait.

Try This

- Show you are sitting on the horse while riding.
- Be the horse doing the cantering.
- Change direction. First as the horse, then as the rider.
- Change level. First as the horse, then as the rider.
- Change head focus with each cantering step.

From *Building More Dances* by Susan McGreevy-Nichols, Helene Scheff, and Marty Sprague, 2001, Champaign, IL: Human Kinetics.

MORE
Sport and Game Movements

Boxing

Try This

- Box with one hand behind your back.
- Box without moving your feet.
- Box, moving in a circle.
- Go against a much shorter person.
- Quickly dodge your opponent while trying to make a hit.

From *Building More Dances* by Susan McGreevy-Nichols, Helene Scheff, and Marty Sprague, 2001, Champaign, IL: Human Kinetics.

MORE
Sport and Game Movements

Paddling

Try This

- Paddle in a circle.
- Paddle with one oar.
- Paddle, changing sides.
- Paddle, lifting your arms up between each stroke.
- Paddle while flat on your back.

From *Building More Dances* by Susan McGreevy-Nichols, Helene Scheff, and Marty Sprague, 2001, Champaign, IL: Human Kinetics.

Doing a Handstand

Try This

- Lean against a wall.
- Bend your knees.
- Pirouette (a turn on one hand or foot).
- Push up from standing on your head.
- Quickly pick up one hand.

From *Building More Dances* by Susan McGreevy-Nichols, Helene Scheff, and Marty Sprague, 2001, Champaign, IL: Human Kinetics.

Doing Jumping Jacks

Try This

- Jump forward and backward instead of opening and closing side to side. Arms stay the same.
- Explore ways to move your arms.
- Add a half turn to each jump.
- Add a quarter turn to each jump.
- Do them at a low level.

From *Building More Dances* by Susan McGreevy-Nichols, Helene Scheff, and Marty Sprague, 2001, Champaign, IL: Human Kinetics.

Exploring Internal Dimensions of Length, Width, and Depth

Description: Consider the torso is three-dimensional and may be experienced head to tail (length); side to side (width), and front to back (depth).

Try This

- When breathing in, really make your torso expand from top to bottom, moving away from center. Then shrink your torso as you breathe out top and bottom, moving toward center. Now really focus on breathing from one side to the other and from the front to the back.

- Experiment with the idea of growing and shrinking in the following positions: lying down, sitting, and standing.

From *Building More Dances* by Susan McGreevy-Nichols, Helene Scheff, and Marty Sprague, 2001, Champaign, IL: Human Kinetics.

Exploring Basic Movement Relationships

Description: Exploring the movements possible in different places in the body and the relationships between these areas: upper body/lower body, right side/left side, center of the body/edges of the body (central/peripheral).

Try This

- Explore what type of movements are possible in these body places: shaking, swaying, swinging, and circling.

- Let a movement start in one body place and travel to another place: upper to lower, right to left, center to edges, and the opposite directions for each pair of areas.

- Start one type of movement in one body place and add another type of movement in another body place. For example, create a rhythmic "beat" in the lower part of your body and swing your upper body.

From *Building More Dances* by Susan McGreevy-Nichols, Helene Scheff, and Marty Sprague, 2001, Champaign, IL: Human Kinetics.

Elements That Change Movement

Body

Exploring Movements Possible at Joints

Description: Different types of movements are possible at differently constructed joints: flexion/extension (bending and straightening); inward and outward rotation; abduction (moving away from centerline of body); and adduction (moving toward centerline of body).

Try This

- Do a joint survey, exploring what types of movements different joints of your body can do.
- Create a body-part dance by letting different body parts have a "conversation" with one another (elbow talks to foot, hand talks to head, and so on).

From *Building More Dances* by Susan McGreevy-Nichols, Helene Scheff, and Marty Sprague, 2001, Champaign, IL: Human Kinetics.

Elements That Change Movement

Body

Exploring Dynamic Balance

Description: Balance (the body's staying in a certain shape) is a *dynamic* action. In other words, muscles in your body are constantly making small movements to help you keep your balance. So there is no such thing as being perfectly "frozen" in a balance.

Try This

- Standing on both feet with your eyes closed, notice that, after a while, small swaying movements start. Try this balancing on one leg. Try other off-center shapes.
- Use this knowledge to create wobbling or tightrope-walking movements.

From *Building More Dances* by Susan McGreevy-Nichols, Helene Scheff, and Marty Sprague, 2001, Champaign, IL: Human Kinetics.

Elements That Change Movement

Space

Bending, Stretching, and Twisting Limbs and Trunk

Description: The limbs and trunk are capable of moving in space differently while lying down, sitting, kneeling, standing, or changing positions.

Try This

- Find bending, stretching, and twisting movements while lying down, sitting, kneeling, standing, or changing positions.

- Create a "changing-positions dance," including bending, stretching, and twisting movements.

From *Building More Dances* by Susan McGreevy-Nichols, Helene Scheff, and Marty Sprague, 2001, Champaign, IL: Human Kinetics.

MORE

Elements That Change Movement

Space

Exploring Kinesphere

Description: This is space that the body can move into, through, and around. This space is three-dimensional, having length, width, and depth.

Try This

- Reach body parts into space by "spoking" (making direct lines from point to point in space), "arcing" (making a single curved "path" from point to point in space), and "carving" (letting the body part carve imaginary pathways in space).

- Let the movements just described carry the body into locomotion.

From *Building More Dances* by Susan McGreevy-Nichols, Helene Scheff, and Marty Sprague, 2001, Champaign, IL: Human Kinetics.

MORE Elements That Change Movement

Space

Gathering and Scattering

Description: Movement can be described as *gathering* (coming into the body) or *scattering* (going away from the body).

Try This

- Explore movements that demonstrate gathering and scattering.
- Explore other movements that might demonstrate folding/unfolding, possessing/pushing away, sharing with/excluding from.

From *Building More Dances* by Susan McGreevy-Nichols, Helene Scheff, and Marty Sprague, 2001, Champaign, IL: Human Kinetics.

MORE Elements That Change Movement

Space

Exploring Locomotion

Description: This includes any movement that can help you travel from place to place, such as walking, rolling, jumping, cartwheeling, creeping, crawling, and the like.

Try This

- Travel through an imaginary obstacle course that calls for different types of locomotive movements.
- Use these locomotive movements to travel in different floor patterns, such as straight lines, angles, curves, circles, and so on.

From *Building More Dances* by Susan McGreevy-Nichols, Helene Scheff, and Marty Sprague, 2001, Champaign, IL: Human Kinetics.

MORE Elements That Change Movement

Space

Exploring Planes

Description: Movements in space can be said to occupy *planes* or combinations of these planes: The *vertical* plane can be described as someone moving within a door frame while doing a cartwheel. The *sagittal* plane can be described as someone wheeling a bicycle while doing front-to-back movements or somersaults. The *horizontal* plane can be described as someone moving across a flat surface, such as washing a table.

Try This

- Explore movements you can do in these planes.
- Combine movements from each plane into longer movement phrases.

From *Building More Dances* by Susan McGreevy-Nichols, Helene Scheff, and Marty Sprague, 2001, Champaign, IL: Human Kinetics.

MORE Elements That Change Movement

Space

Exploring Levels

Description: You may move through space at three different levels: high, middle, and low.

Try This

- Discover movements you can do at each level, including some locomotion.
- Create a little dance at each level.
- Make a larger dance by creating transitions from one level's dance into another level's dance, combining the dances.

From *Building More Dances* by Susan McGreevy-Nichols, Helene Scheff, and Marty Sprague, 2001, Champaign, IL: Human Kinetics.

MORE
Elements That Change Movement

Effort

Exploring Flow

Description: The way the body moves, the quality, or in other words, "how" you move, is controlled by the *attitude* you have toward the movement's energy. Attitude toward flow can be called *bound* (controlled) or *free* (uncontrolled).

Try This

- Create different imaginary environments that call for different efforts, such as (1) moving through a thick "mud-like" atmosphere (bound flow) and (2) moving as if there was no muscle control necessary, either flailing or "going with the flow" (free flow).

- Create and do a real-life activity that calls for free and bound flow. Change the activity's movement from literal (real-life) to abstract. Make sure you emphasize the effort of flow.

From *Building More Dances* by Susan McGreevy-Nichols, Helene Scheff, and Marty Sprague, 2001, Champaign, IL: Human Kinetics.

MORE
Elements That Change Movement

Effort

Exploring Space

Description: The way that the body moves, the quality, or in other words, "how" you move, is controlled by the *attitude* you have toward the movement's energy. Attitude toward space may be called *direct* (the movement has a single focus) or *indirect* (the movement has many focuses).

Try This

- Create different imaginary environments that call for different efforts, such as (1) a situation that only asks you to do one thing at a time (threading a needle uses *direct space*) and (2) a situation that asks you to do too many things at the same time (multi-tasking uses *indirect space*).

- Create and do a real-life activity that calls for direct and indirect space. Change the activity's movement from literal (real-life) to abstract. Make sure you emphasize the effort of space.

From *Building More Dances* by Susan McGreevy-Nichols, Helene Scheff, and Marty Sprague, 2001, Champaign, IL: Human Kinetics.

MORE Elements That Change Movement

Effort

Exploring Time

Description: The way the body moves, the quality, or in other words, "how" you move, is controlled by the *attitude* you have toward the movement's energy. Attitude toward time can be called *sudden* (showing urgency or anxiety) or *sustained* (showing a relaxed, easygoing feeling).

Try This

- Create different imaginary environments or activities that call for different efforts, such as (1) being somewhere that gives you an urgent, anxious feeling (sudden time) and (2) being somewhere you may be relaxed and not worried (sustained time).

- Create and do a real-life activity that calls for sudden and sustained time. Change the activity's movement from literal (real-life) to abstract. Make sure you emphasize the effort of time.

From *Building More Dances* by Susan McGreevy-Nichols, Helene Scheff, and Marty Sprague, 2001, Champaign, IL: Human Kinetics.

MORE Elements That Change Movement

Effort

Exploring Weight

Description: The way the body moves, the quality, or in other words, "how" you move, is controlled by the *attitude* you have toward the movement's energy. Attitude toward weight can be called *strong* (expending much energy) or *light* (using a fine touch).

Try This

- Create different imaginary environments or activities that call for different efforts, such as (1) doing something that requires a great deal of force (strong weight) or (2) doing something that calls for careful, delicate attention (light weight).

- Create and do a real-life activity that calls for strong and light. Change the activity's movement from literal (real-life) to abstract. Make sure you emphasize the effort of weight.

From *Building More Dances* by Susan McGreevy-Nichols, Helene Scheff, and Marty Sprague, 2001, Champaign, IL: Human Kinetics.

Elements That Change Movement

MORE

Effort

Exploring Effort Actions II (Light Weight)

Description: Combine different aspects of effort (space, time, and weight) to create the basic effort actions. Examples using light weight include the following: (1) floating: indirect space, light weight, sustained time; (2) gliding: direct space, light weight, sustained time; (3) dabbing: direct space, light weight, sudden time; (4) flicking: indirect space, light weight, sudden time.

Try This

- Create and write a story using the above effort action words.
- Make a dance retelling this story, demonstrating the above effort actions.

From *Building More Dances* by Susan McGreevy-Nichols, Helene Scheff, and Marty Sprague, 2001, Champaign, IL: Human Kinetics.

Elements That Change Movement

MORE

Effort

Exploring Effort Actions I (Strong Weight)

Description: Combine different aspects of effort (space, time, and weight) to create the basic effort actions. Examples using strong weight include the following: (1) punching: direct space, strong weight, sudden time; (2) slashing: indirect space, strong weight, sudden time; (3) wringing: indirect space, strong weight, sustained time; (4) pressing: direct space, strong weight, sustained time.

Try This

- Create and write a story using the above effort action words.
- Make a dance retelling this story, demonstrating the above effort actions.

From *Building More Dances* by Susan McGreevy-Nichols, Helene Scheff, and Marty Sprague, 2001, Champaign, IL: Human Kinetics.

MORE
Dance Techniques and Basic Movements

Tap, Jazz

Basic Movement—Locomotor

Doing the Suzie Q

Description: In two counts, cross and step left foot in front of right, then step right foot to side, while twisting open on the heel of the left foot.

Try This

- Do a whole line of Suzie Qs.
- Reverse the direction.
- Perform them in a circle.
- Hold your hands together and move them in opposition to your body. When your right foot crosses over to the left, your hands cross your body to the right.

From *Building More Dances* by Susan McGreevy-Nichols, Helene Scheff, and Marty Sprague, 2001, Champaign, IL: Human Kinetics.

MORE
Dance Techniques and Basic Movements

Tap

Basic Movement—Locomotor

Flapping

Description: Brush one foot forward and then place that foot down in front of the other foot, shifting weight.

Try This

- Do step with alternating feet while traveling forward.
- Do the step on the balls of your feet.
- Do the step moving backward.
- Don't make the weight shift; instead, use the same foot repeatedly.

From *Building More Dances* by Susan McGreevy-Nichols, Helene Scheff, and Marty Sprague, 2001, Champaign, IL: Human Kinetics.

Brushing

Description:

1. Stand on one leg. At the same time, bend the other leg at the knee.
2. Extend the raised leg forward, hitting the floor with the ball of your foot.

Try This

- Extend your leg to the side.
- Propel your leg to the back.
- Put your raised leg down after the brush. (This is called *flapping*.)
- Brush your foot to the back after it goes to the front. (This is called *shuffling*.)
- Vary the height of the working leg.

From *Building More Dances* by Susan McGreevy-Nichols, Helene Scheff, and Marty Sprague, 2001, Champaign, IL: Human Kinetics.

Waltz Clogging (Doing the "Bojangles" Step)

Description:

1. Flap your right foot (brush, step).
2. Shuffle your left foot (brush forward, brush back).
3. Change from the ball of one foot to that of the other (left foot step, right foot step).

Try This

- Alternate feet.
- Perform in a circle.
- Perform the whole combination on the balls of your feet.
- Add arm movements.

From *Building More Dances* by Susan McGreevy-Nichols, Helene Scheff, and Marty Sprague, 2001, Champaign, IL: Human Kinetics.

MORE

Dance Techniques and Basic Movements

Ethnic

Basic Movement—Nonlocomotor

Digging

Description: While standing on one foot, place the heel of the other foot on the floor, keeping the foot flexed.

Try This

- Place the heel in different places.
- Make a rhythmical pattern by tapping the heel.
- Combine digging with a step.

From *Building More Dances* by Susan McGreevy-Nichols, Helene Scheff, and Marty Sprague, 2001, Champaign, IL: Human Kinetics.

MORE

Dance Techniques and Basic Movements

Tap

Basic Movement—Nonlocomotor

Shuffling and Stamping

Description:

- Using the ball of your foot, brush your foot forward and then backward, making two sounds.
- Place the raised foot down with energy right next to the leg you are standing on.

Try This

- Alternate feet.
- Travel forward while alternating feet.
- Travel backward while alternating feet.
- Clap in between the shuffle and the stamp.
- Change the rhythm.

From *Building More Dances* by Susan McGreevy-Nichols, Helene Scheff, and Marty Sprague, 2001, Champaign, IL: Human Kinetics.

MORE
Dance Techniques and Basic Movements

Vernacular Dance

Basic Movement—Locomotor

Dancing the Charleston

Description:

1. Step out on right foot.
2. Kick left foot up to the front and slightly across the right leg.
3. Step back on left foot.
4. Touch the right toe behind the left leg.

Try This

- Reverse the step.
- Put the opposite hand toward the leg that is raised up in the air.
- Bend over when the right leg goes back.
- Add a hop when you kick the leg forward.

From *Building More Dances* by Susan McGreevy-Nichols, Helene Scheff, and Marty Sprague, 2001, Champaign, IL: Human Kinetics.

MORE
Dance Techniques and Basic Movements

Tap

Basic Movement—Locomotor

Doing the Cramp Roll (Drum Roll)

Description: Say, "toe, toe, heel drop, heel drop," in four counts.

1. Count 1: Place ball of right foot on the ground.
2. Count 2: Place ball of left foot on the ground next to the right (you should now be on the balls of both feet).
3. Count 3: Let the heel of the right foot drop to the ground, making a sound.
4. Count 4: Let the heel of the left foot drop to the ground, making a sound.

Try This

- Reverse to left.
- Change speed.
- Travel forward.
- Make a quarter turn with each cramp roll.
- Before the start of each cramp roll, brush the lead foot forward before placing it on its ball (on the "and" count of 1).

From *Building More Dances* by Susan McGreevy-Nichols, Helene Scheff, and Marty Sprague, 2001, Champaign, IL: Human Kinetics.

Doing the Polka (Regular Step)

Description: Say, "one, two, three, rest," in four counts.

1. Hop on left foot on the end of the first count.
2. Step right foot out to side on count one.
3. Close left foot to right on count two, and step with right foot on count three.
4. Rest on fourth count.

Try This

- Do the step on other side, hopping onto right foot first.
- Do the step with a partner.
- Take two steps to make a revolution, and keep going (like in *The King and I*).

From *Building More Dances* by Susan McGreevy-Nichols, Helene Scheff, and Marty Sprague, 2001, Champaign, IL: Human Kinetics.

Doing the *Pas de Boureé*

Description: Say, "step back, side, front," in three counts.

1. Place the ball of right foot behind the left.
2. Place the ball of left foot out to side of the right.
3. Place the right foot flat on the floor in front of the left and raise the left foot just a bit.

Try This

- Reverse the direction.
- Do the step while turning.
- Add arm movements.
- Start with the first foot going in front of the standing foot.
- Combine one plain *pas de Boureé* with one turning.

From *Building More Dances* by Susan McGreevy-Nichols, Helene Scheff, and Marty Sprague, 2001, Champaign, IL: Human Kinetics.

Chasse–Galloping

Description:

1. Step out on one foot.
2. Bring the other foot in to meet first foot, taking weight off the first foot in the air as it transfers to the second foot.

Try This

- Go sideways but face forward.
- Go forward but face sideways.
- Travel in a circle.
- Explore high, middle, and low levels.
- Explore changing the rhythm.

From *Building More Dances* by Susan McGreevy-Nichols, Helene Scheff, and Marty Sprague, 2001, Champaign, IL: Human Kinetics.

Doing the Allemande (One-Handed Full or Half Turn)

Description: Couple stands close, locks bent elbows, and wraps fingers around each other's hands.

Try This

- Skip while turning.
- Hop on one foot while turning.
- Touch elbows instead of locking them.
- Explore high, middle, and low levels while turning.

From *Building More Dances* by Susan McGreevy-Nichols, Helene Scheff, and Marty Sprague, 2001, Champaign, IL: Human Kinetics.

Doing Jumping Jacks (Echappé)

Description:

1. From a neutral position with feet together, bend knees, then spring into the air.
2. Open legs to the side and land with feet apart on slightly bent knees.
3. Spring into the air, closing feet.
4. Land with feet together with knees slightly bent.

Try This

- Open feet so that one foot is in front of you and the other is behind.
- Land on one leg in the open position.
- Match your arms to legs.
- Make arms move opposite to legs.

From *Building More Dances* by Susan McGreevy-Nichols, Helene Scheff, and Marty Sprague, 2001, Champaign, IL: Human Kinetics.

Doing the Pas de Bas–Pas de Basque

Description: Say, "one, two, three," in three counts.

1. Step right foot to the side.
2. Place left foot well in front of right foot.
3. Close the right foot to the left.

Try This

- Use the other foot.
- Plié, bending the knee on the first foot.
- Accent the step by making a loud sound with the last foot (stamp).
- Do the step going backward (reversing direction).

From *Building More Dances* by Susan McGreevy-Nichols, Helene Scheff, and Marty Sprague, 2001, Champaign, IL: Human Kinetics.

Doing the Cakewalk

Description: This dance was done by slaves in the deep south of the United States, made up of varying steps. See the two below.

1. Bring one knee up and prance to other leg, keeping knees high when in the air.

2. Step out, step other leg in, and step out again with the first leg, all while making arm circles with the arm of the lead foot.

Try This

- Prance in a big circle.
- Clap a tambourine while prancing.
- Do the second step as if you were scrubbing the floor.
- Do the second step as if you were washing a high window.

From *Building More Dances* by Susan McGreevy-Nichols, Helene Scheff, and Marty Sprague, 2001, Champaign, IL: Human Kinetics.

Doing the Siva Dance

Description:

1. Bend your knees (plié). Tilt your head slightly to one side.

2. Move sideways by first moving both your heels to the right, then sliding your toes to the right. Keep repeating this movement.

3. Move your hands in a circular motion, weaving patterns in the air.

Try This

- Think of a story you would like to tell.
- Use your hands to tell it.

From *Building More Dances* by Susan McGreevy-Nichols, Helene Scheff, and Marty Sprague, 2001, Champaign, IL: Human Kinetics.

MORE **Dance Techniques and Basic Movements**

Tap, Jazz, Folk, Ethnic

Basic Movement—Locomotor

Doing the Chug Step

Description:

1. Start with both feet together, knees slightly bent.
2. Move forward without coming off the floor.
3. Using the same technique, move backward.

Try This

- Do the step on one foot.
- Do the step on one foot while extending and pulling in the raised leg.
- Swing the arms while performing the step.

From *Building More Dances* by Susan McGreevy-Nichols, Helene Scheff, and Marty Sprague, 2001, Champaign, IL: Human Kinetics.

MORE **Dance Techniques and Basic Movements**

Vernacular

Basic Movement—Locomotor

Doing the Black Bottom

Description:

1. With knees bent, stamp feet. Hands are on the knees.
2. With knees together and bent, sway them from side to side, letting your toes guide the movement.
3. With knees bent, push right hip to the side and pat the hip with hand on same side.

Try This

- Do number 1 while clapping hands in a rhythmical pattern.
- Do number 2, making hands go in opposite directions (when knees go right, hands go left). Explore different hand motions.
- Do number 3 while making a circle around yourself.

From *Building More Dances* by Susan McGreevy-Nichols, Helene Scheff, and Marty Sprague, 2001, Champaign, IL: Human Kinetics.

MORE
Dance Techniques and Basic Movements

Character, Folk

Basic Movement—Locomotor

Doing the Mazurka

Description:

1. Step left (with slight stamp).
2. Bring right foot up to left and transfer weight heavily.
3. Hop on the right foot.

Try This

- Use other leg.
- Slide the first foot.
- Devise arm movements to go with the step.

From *Building More Dances* by Susan McGreevy-Nichols, Helene Scheff, and Marty Sprague, 2001, Champaign, IL: Human Kinetics.

MORE
Dance Techniques and Basic Movements

Folk, Square

Basic Movement—Locomotor

Doing the Schottische

Description:

1. Step left, transferring weight with each move.
2. Step right.
3. Step left.
4. Hop on left.

Try This

- Start with the right leg.
- Clap when you hop.
- Move forward on all three steps.
- Make a quarter turn on the hop.
- Combine the bulleted items above, linking the order and then rearranging the order.

From *Building More Dances* by Susan McGreevy-Nichols, Helene Scheff, and Marty Sprague, 2001, Champaign, IL: Human Kinetics.

MORE
Dance Techniques and Basic Movements

Tap, Jazz, Folk

Basic Movement—Locomotor

Scuffing

Description: Brush one heel forward, making a sound.

Try This

- Bend the knee of the leg you are standing on while scuffing.
- Cross both hands across your body while scuffing, opposite to your leg (when your leg goes right, your arms go left).
- Make the scuffing leg go to the side.

From *Building More Dances* by Susan McGreevy-Nichols, Helene Scheff, and Marty Sprague, 2001, Champaign, IL: Human Kinetics.

MORE
Dance Techniques and Basic Movements

Folk

Basic Movement—Locomotor

Dancing the Hora
(Chain Dance of Israel)

Description:

Counts 1 and 2. Step to right with right foot, and kick left leg across right.

Counts 3 and 4. Step to left with your left foot, then kick right leg across left.

Counts 5 through 8: "Grapevine" to left, starting by crossing with right foot (do four steps total).

Try This

- In a group, make a big circle with bodies facing in, holding hands at middle level, and keep repeating step.
- Make a chain and weave different floor patterns.
- Make a heavy stamping sound on the odd-numbered counts.
- Make a heavy stamping sound on the even-numbered counts.

From *Building More Dances* by Susan McGreevy-Nichols, Helene Scheff, and Marty Sprague, 2001, Champaign, IL: Human Kinetics.

MORE
Dance Techniques and Basic Movements

Folk

Basic Movement—Locomotor

Adding the Heel-Toe Step to the Polka

Description:

1. Hop on right foot with left heel extended to the side.
2. Hop on right foot, crossing left foot over right arch.
3. Do a regular polka step (hop on right foot, step out with left, pull right foot in, step out on left).

Try This

- Reverse movements by starting on the other foot.
- Do two whole steps to make one revolution (complete circle).
- Cross hands with a partner while doing the steps.

From *Building More Dances* by Susan McGreevy-Nichols, Helene Scheff, and Marty Sprague, 2001, Champaign, IL: Human Kinetics.

MORE
Dance Techniques and Basic Movements

Folk, Square, Vernacular

Basic Movement—Locomotor

Doing the Two-Step

Description:

Count 1: Step out on right foot.

Count and: Step together with left foot on the "and."

Count 2: Step out on right foot.

Counts 3 & 4: Pause, pause.

Try This

- Face a partner, holding hands. Have one partner move forward as the other moves backward.
- Alternate steps, making triangular floor patterns.
- Explore arm movements to add.

From *Building More Dances* by Susan McGreevy-Nichols, Helene Scheff, and Marty Sprague, 2001, Champaign, IL: Human Kinetics.

MORE
Dance Techniques and Basic Movements

Vernacular, Ballroom

Basic Movement—Locomotor

Doing the Castle Walk

Description:

1. Step out on right foot.
2. Step out on left foot.
3. Point right foot forward and then backward.

Try This

- Move arms in opposition to the walk. In other words, when the right leg is forward, the left arm is forward, and when the left leg is forward, the right arm is forward.
- Nest together with a partner and step as one person.
- Do the step moving backward.

From *Building More Dances* by Susan McGreevy-Nichols, Helene Scheff, and Marty Sprague, 2001, Champaign, IL: Human Kinetics.

MORE
Dance Techniques and Basic Movements

Jazz, Modern

Basic Movement—Nonlocomotor

Doing Isolations

Description: This describes how to do an isolation of the hip.

1. Stand in a comfortable stance.
2. Move one hip to the side without moving any other part of your body.
3. Move the hip back to the starting position.

Try This

- Move only your shoulder.
- Move only your rib cage to the side.
- Move rib cage toward the front.

From *Building More Dances* by Susan McGreevy-Nichols, Helene Scheff, and Marty Sprague, 2001, Champaign, IL: Human Kinetics.

MORE Dance Techniques and Basic Movements

Folk, Ethnic

Basic Movement—Locomotor

Walking (Cambodian Dance III)

Description:

- Bend your knees, put your heels together, and turn your toes outward. (*Note:* This is called the first position in ballet.)

- Hold your hands with extended thumb and index finger on the same hand almost touching.

- Sway slightly back and forth, and, placing the heel of your right foot against the toe of your left foot, step down on your right foot. Reverse the procedure by placing the heel of your left foot against the toe of your right foot.

Try This

- Do some hand gestures while walking.
- Walk backward.
- Make a floor pattern of a rectangle.

From *Building More Dances* by Susan McGreevy-Nichols, Helene Scheff, and Marty Sprague, 2001, Champaign, IL: Human Kinetics.

MORE Dance Techniques and Basic Movements

Folk

Basic Movement—Nonlocomotor

Offering, Smiling, and Crying (Cambodian Dance II)

Description:

1. Stretch out your thumb and index finger on each hand until they almost touch.

2. Curve back the other fingers.

3. To smile, cross your thumb and index finger over your mouth. To cry, move the fingers held in the same position across your eyes.

Try This

- Explore gestures with hands in the same positions as described above to mean other things.

- Combine these gestures to tell a short story.

- Sit on the floor.

From *Building More Dances* by Susan McGreevy-Nichols, Helene Scheff, and Marty Sprague, 2001, Champaign, IL: Human Kinetics.

MORE Dance Techniques and Basic Movements

Folk

Basic Movement—Nonlocomotor

Doing the Sampieh (Cambodian Dance I)

Description: A *sampieh* is a salute showing respect.

1. Stand upright.

2. Touch your knees with your hands, then lift your hands to chest level.

3. Place your palms together with your fingers curved back and your thumbs pointing outward.

4. Raise the thumbs to your forehead.

Try This

• Do this while squatting.

• Do this in slow motion.

• Create a different salute, done in the same style.

• Make a short dance, combining several salutes.

From *Building More Dances* by Susan McGreevy-Nichols, Helene Scheff, and Marty Sprague, 2001, Champaign, IL: Human Kinetics.

MORE Dance Techniques and Basic Movements

Folk

Basic Movement—Locomotor

Doing the Hula

Description:

1. Start with feet together, knees slightly bent.

2. Step to the right, swaying hips to the left in a slightly circular way.

3. Pull the left foot in to barely touching the ground—without transferring weight.

Try This

• Make two hula steps to right and two hula steps to left.

• Rotate hands while doing the hula steps.

• Make up hand gestures to tell a story while doing the hula.

From *Building More Dances* by Susan McGreevy-Nichols, Helene Scheff, and Marty Sprague, 2001, Champaign, IL: Human Kinetics.